THIS HEBREW LORD

REVISED EDITION

John Shelby Spong

1817

Harper & Row, Publishers, San Francisco

Cambridge, Hagerstown, New York, Philadelphia, Washington
London, Mexico City, São Paulo, Singapore, Sydney

REVISED EDITION

Library of Congress Cataloging-in-Publication Data

Spong, John Shelby.
  This Hebrew Lord.

  Bibliography: p.
  1. Jesus Christ—Person and offices. 2. Christianity and other religions—Judaism. 3. Judaism—Relations—Christianity. I. Title.
BT202.S667 1988 232 86-43020
ISBN 0-06-254806-9 (pbk.)

88 89 90 91 MPC 10 9 8 7 6 5 4 3 2 1

FOR JOAN
whose love creates and re-creates my life, and

FOR ELLEN, KATHARINE, JAQUELIN
whose lives are the source of our deepest joy.

Contents

Preface to the Revised Edition

A B O O K, like a child, grows up and has an independent life of its own. This book was written in 1973.
It went through four printings and sold more copies than
any other book I've ever written. After fourteen years, including a brief stint "OP," it is being given new life
again, not the life of a new printing but the life of a revised edition newly edited, somewhat updated, and above
all with an inclusiveness of language to which the author
was simply not sensitive in 1973. As this new edition
came into being this author had the wonderful opportunity to correct some errors, change some words, and launch
this book on perhaps some new adventures.

In its fourteen-year pilgrimage through existence, *This
Hebrew Lord* has been responsible for two life-changing
episodes for its author. These episodes have in turn been
major events in the life of the church in America, of
which the author is a part.

The first episode occurred in 1974 when a rabbi from

a Reform synagogue in Richmond was attending a cocktail party at the home of one of his neighbors. A copy of *This Hebrew Lord* was on the table in the living room during the party. The rabbi, whose name was Jack Daniel Spiro, saw the book, was intrigued by the title, and borrowed the book. A week later he called my office, which at that time was the rector's study at St. Paul's Episcopal Church in Richmond, Virginia. "I have just read your book," he said, "and I've never read a book by a Christian that paid such homage to the Jewish tradition, but I disagree with your conclusions."

I was both flattered and amused. "Of course you disagree," I responded. "If you didn't you would have to be baptized, and there are very few synagogues where a baptized rabbi would be well received."

We laughed and discovered even over the phone an intellectual and emotional rapport. "I would like to engage you and your book in a debate in front of the members of Temple Beth Ahabah at our Sabbath eve services," the rabbi continued. I accepted immediately, expanding the format to include not just sessions before the congregation in the synagogue on Sabbath eve, but also before the congregation of St. Paul's Church on Sunday mornings. So we went to work on what was to be for me a turning point of life.

For eight sessions—an introduction at the synagogue and a conclusion at the church, plus three Friday evenings at Temple Beth Ahabah and three Sunday mornings at St. Paul's Church—Jack Spiro and I conducted what came to be called a "Dialogue: In Search of Jewish-Christian Understanding." It was a remarkable event. The crowds at the synagogue were like Rosh Hashanah and the crowds at the church were like Easter. A rabbi standing with integrity inside the faith tradition of Judaism sought to break through Christian prejudices and stereotypes and invite Christians to see the beauty and power of Judaism. A priest standing with integrity inside the faith tradition of Christianity sought to break through Jewish prejudices and stereotypes and invite Jews to see the beauty and power of Christianity.

This dialogue captured the city of Richmond as few religious events have ever done. Both the rabbi and I became public figures and began, perhaps inevitably, to be shot at by our detractors. The Orthodox Jews attacked the rabbi; the fundamentalist Christians attacked me. Because there were many more fundamentalist Christians than Orthodox Jews in Richmond, I starred for three months in the letters-to-the-editor section of the Richmond *Times-Dispatch,* usually being attacked with vengeance. The national religious press picked this up and my orthodoxy, or personal lack of it, was debated in Christian circles around the nation. Members of one very conservative Southern Baptist church even picketed St. Paul's Church, carrying placards that suggested that I did not believe the Bible literally (they were correct), and that I didn't believe in Jesus (they were incorrect). Abusive mail was frequent. The most amusing letter came after a remark on television in which I said that Rabbi Spiro had become such a close personal friend during this dialogue that if I were to die I would want him to be one of my pallbearers. "I hope it will not be long until the rabbi can serve you in that capacity" were the words of a letter received two days later.

This dialogue launched me on a study of other great religious systems, including a dialogue I had in India in 1984 with three Hindu scholars. All of this was my first great inheritance from *This Hebrew Lord,* a powerful book for me whose independent life continued to affect my life in ways outside my control.

The second great contribution to my life of *This Hebrew Lord* came in 1976. On March 6 of that year I was elected Bishop of Newark (northern New Jersey). In the Episcopal Church, ratification of a bishop's election must be received from a majority of the standing committees made up of elected clergy and laity from each diocese in America and a majority of the bishops having jurisdiction in America. Normally this is a pro forma requirement, but because of *This Hebrew Lord* it was not to be so in my case. A group of some seventy conservative Episcopalians organized a campaign to prevent the ratification of my election by the Diocese of Newark. They attacked my Christology as heretical, and my theology as unorthodox. They quoted passages from *This Hebrew Lord.* Once again I found myself in a storm of controversy being debated in every Episcopal diocese in America. When I was finally confirmed (only thirteen dioceses voted no), it was clear that theological controversy would always be associated with my career. I resented that then, but I have come to appreciate it greatly today.

With the publication of *This Hebrew Lord,* I began to stand in the American Episcopal Church in a place very similar to that once occupied by John A. T. Robinson in the Church of England, whose works the reader will soon discover were powerfully influential on my development as a priest and as a scholar. I am a bishop who dares to be a scholar, who welcomes theological controversy, who is frequently published, and whose life is dedicated to the dialogue between Christianity and the secular world, which includes a serious attempt to learn from both the secular spirit and the non-Christian religions of the world.

Like John Robinson, I seem to be the bane of the existence of those Christians, including some bishops, who want their beliefs to be certain, their Christianity to be unchallenged, their Bibles and Creeds to be taken literally. And all of this I owe to this volume, *This Hebrew Lord.*

I must thank those people who assisted me in preparing this new and revised edition. First, to the Reverend Elizabeth Maxwell, the rector of St. Matthew's Church in Paramus, New Jersey, and a representative of that wonderful new group of women priests who are changing the shape of our church, for assisting me in removing the sexist language to which I was in fact not sensitive when the book was first written. The male God and a humanity that seems to include only men are both doomed in a church that now sees a new and inclusive God and a humanity that transcends the limitations of yesterday. Women priests have not yet been elected to the office of bishop in our church, but that will come before this edition has sold out. It is as inevitable and should be as welcomed as the dawn that wakens a new day. Liz Maxwell will be one of the giants among the church's clergy in the decade of the nineties.

To Wanda Hollenbeck, Susan Ayres, and Barbara Festa, who typed the new edition, reproduced it for several editing procedures, and assisted in so many ways, go my special thanks. This is the second book of mine on which Wanda has worked and my appreciation of her knows no bounds. She is marvelously capable on the word processor and her pleasant manner and trustworthy personality make her an invaluable part of my life.

Finally, I wish to thank my staff in the Diocese of Newark—the Archdeacons Denise G. Haines, James W. H. Sell, and Leslie C. Smith and the Chief Financial and Administrative Officers John Zinn and Christine M.

Barney—for creating in Cathedral House a community that is productive, life-giving, and full of both joy and integrity as we share together in the task of leadership in the ministry of the Diocese of Newark. Because of them, writing, editing, and publishing become a pleasure, not a chore, even though this avocation of the one who is their bishop clearly puts additional demands upon their lives.

The book was dedicated originally to the members of my primary family and that dedication is joyfully continued in the new edition. However, fourteen years change life dramatically. My then young daughters are today grown women involved in careers in banking, law, and science. These now mature women have helped to deliver me from the male chauvinism of my youth. Our cat, Hermann, mentioned in the original preface, now rests in peace underneath the holly tree at our New Jersey home. All of the members of this family have made their contributions to this book directly and indirectly and that contribution I gratefully acknowledge.

Shalom
JOHN SHELBY SPONG

Newark, New Jersey
January, 1988

Preface

T H I S book is the story of a struggle that was both personal and theological. It was a struggle to translate the power in Jesus of Nazareth into the categories of our day. It is not offered as a definitive Christology but as a personal witness. It is a dialogue in which I will be revealed to my reader, and my reader will inevitably have to interact with me.

This book has been under preparation for years as its corpus will reveal. Parts of it have been given as lectures in many churches of this land and at church conference centers at Kanuga in North Carolina and Hemlock Haven in Virginia. One chapter (11) has been substantially published as a separate article in *The Episcopalian*, April, 1973. Most specifically, it reflects my life in St. Paul's Church, Richmond, Virginia, where I serve a congregation that possesses unusual vitality, intellectual power, and deep inner resources of life. The members of this congregation, time after time, make my life new, and in response to their demands I am constantly being called to heretofore unknown horizons. For the privilege of this ministry I am grateful. One of my predecessors as rector of St. Paul's was my former teacher, Walter Russell Bowie. I can never walk in his footsteps but I would like to think I walk in his shadow. The issues facing the church in my day are not unlike the ones he had to face. He made a vital difference from his position at St. Paul's. I hope I can do the same.

I need to acknowledge many of the people who have helped me prepare this volume. First my thanks go to my administrative assistant, Lucy Boswell Negus, who has corrected my spelling, shaped my sentences, helped clarify my thoughts, and encouraged my embarking on this enterprise. Second, I was assisted by three very gifted readers, Jean Leonard LeRoy, Cyane Hoar Lowden, and Carter Donnan McDowell, all of whom spent many hours working on the original and subsequent manuscripts.

Third, members of my staff at St. Paul's aided me immeasurably. Mary Kuehl Barden typed the first copy and drew diagrams for the illustrations; Felicia Huffer Lightfoot, Walton Speake Pettit, Raymond Frederick Glover, Eleanor Noble Jackson, Sargeant Herbert Brown, and Carolyn Henna Shelton assisted in many ways, complained very little about the additional work load, and endured me while I suffered the labor pains of this book's birth.

Fourth, Basil Terence and Penny Powell Carmody, who gave me the use of their home for writing while they were out of the city; Betty McLennan Barden, who typed the final copy; Celia Kyle Luxmoore, who worked especially on Chapter 4; Dr. Talbot Selby, Edith Black Zfass, and Mahryam Daniels Aleyshmerni, who assisted with my Greek and Hebrew transliterations; Dr. Frank E. Eakin of the University of Richmond's Department of Religion, who read the manuscript and offered many helpful comments; and my editor, Robert Morgan Gilday, who gave me not only his expertise, but his sense of humor and his gracious friendship; to all these, I am greatly indebted.

My thanks go finally to my family: Joan, my wife; and Ellen, Katharine, and Jaquelin, my daughters. Grace is being loved when you are unlovable, being accepted and forgiven when you least deserve it. I live as the fortunate recipient of this grace from my family, my primary life-giving community. Together, including Hermann the cat, they seem to know just when special care is needed. I do hope that I am to them in some small measure what they seem constantly to be to me.

JOHN SHELBY SPONG

Richmond, Virginia
September 1, 1973

CHRISTPOWER

Look at him!
Look not at his divinity,
        but look, rather, at his freedom.
Look not at the exaggerated tales of his power,
        but look, rather, at his infinite capacity
                                to give himself away.
Look not at the first-century mythology that surrounds him,
        but look, rather, at his courage to be,
                his ability to live
                    the contagious quality of his love.
    Stop your frantic search!
Be still and *know* that this is God:
        this love,
                this freedom,
                    this life,
                        this being;
    and
When you are accepted,
        accept yourself;
When you are forgiven,
        forgive yourself;
When you are loved,
        love yourself.
    Grasp that Christ power
                and
    dare to be yourself!

John Shelby Spong
1973

PART I

✣ ✣ ✣

Developing Hebrew Eyes

1
✣

A Necessary Personal Word

S E V E R A L years ago I was having lunch with a leading businessman in the city of Richmond, Virginia. He was a man who had achieved success far beyond what one would expect at his age, and who was deeply involved in the church. Our conversation turned toward those things we really believed—not just the things we thought we were supposed to believe. In utter honesty he said to me: "I have no trouble believing in God. I am impressed with the wonder and order of creation and life. I have no difficulty with the Christian ethic. I try to act it out, and I think it is the only basis upon which to organize society. But I do have trouble with Jesus. I do not understand how he fits in, or why he is important. I can see him as a teacher and as a great man of insight, but more than that makes no sense to me."

This man was articulating the theological anxiety of our age. He was daring to express what many would-be Christians feel. Ours is an age of doubt, confusion, and lack of certainty. The Jesus we so often hear about in church has little resemblance to the thought forms, the activities, or the mind-set of the twentieth-century world. He is overlaid with myth and superstition. He is victimized by piety and emotions. He is covered with sentimentality and the miraculous. He does not seem real. He makes no contact with our life.

I groped for words to speak to my friend, but his open honesty made it impossible to retreat into the jargon or clichés of my calling. I had to be honest, even though he was raising the most uncomfortable question a clergyperson can face. It was a question that I realized in retrospect I had always attempted to repress, for I was afraid of its consequences. If I could not deal to my own satisfaction with Jesus, the Christ figure, the most basic cornerstone of my profession would have come loose, and my life would be one huge question mark.

I was reminded of a story told about Martin Luther in the early years of the Reformation. Luther realized that the fire he had lit had ignited feelings that not even he was aware existed. The explosion that followed Luther's spark became bigger than anyone could manage or control. The life of the whole world would never again be the same. Luther awoke from his sleep in the middle of the night, and this realization overwhelmed him. He is reported to have cried, "My God, *what if I am wrong!*"

On a much smaller scale, but equally as existential to my life, there came a similar feeling. My whole life, my deepest being, was and is consumed in the practice of the Christian ministry. Suppose, however, that the central foundation of that ministry collapsed. Suppose I could no longer make sense out of Jesus the Christ. Suppose everything I am was based on a superstition, a misunderstanding, an orthodoxy that could not stand the light of day. "My God, *what if I am wrong!*"

I do not suppose I had ever really allowed myself to

search out my Christ before that day. Instead, I had avoided facing this growing anxiety of my generation. I had encapsulated myself in all sorts of religious certainties. But now, somehow, there was no escape. My own latent doubts were triggered by this open, probing question from a friend at lunch. I could not duck the issue. There began for me an intensive probe into the very roots of my faith, the reason for my being. I had to find either a new level of honest commitment or a new profession, a new meaning for my existence. It was at this moment, I suppose, that the seed for this book was germinated.

I cannot remember a time when the church was not a part of my life, yet the early religious attitudes that implanted themselves on my conscious mind were not particularly attractive. My father was an Episcopalian, though he never participated in worship except at Christmas and Easter, and he seemed to resent any financial demand the church made on him. My mother was from a very fundamentalistic Presbyterian family, rigidly moralistic; yet in her own way, she was very loving. She joined my father's church in the hope that he would attend if she went with him. It did not work in improving my father's attendance, but the three children—I being the middle child—were taken to Sunday School regularly.

I can remember winning many medals for perfect attendance, yet when I try to recall the content of those early years in my church, I draw an almost complete blank. I can honestly remember only two things from my entire Sunday School career. I remember being slapped by my fourth-grade teacher for misbehaving. What my misdeed was I have no idea. Only the embarrassment of being slapped remains vivid. My other memory was from the fifth grade, when our subject matter was the Ten Commandments. For some reason that I did not then comprehend, my teacher omitted the seventh commandment. I raised my hand, noting the omission, and said, "Mr. Darrow, what does it mean to 'commit adultery'?" There was an embarrassed silence, and then an animated and flustered response, "You'll learn about that when you get older." To the best of my ability, that is all I can recall of my Sunday School training.

At the proper time in my life I was confirmed. I remember it well, not because of its religious significance, but because it represented for me a kind of adult independence. I was confirmed at a church other than the one of which my parents were members. It was probably the first independent and original deed I ever did. At least my new church was of the same denomination, so it did not create a scandal. It was also the church to which my father had belonged when he was a child, so it did not represent a serious rupture of family tradition. Yet this was in many ways a crucial turning point for me.

Church then came to be filled, for me, with warm feelings. I was first a boy soprano in a very mischievous boys' choir; then an acolyte, greatly enjoying the status of my red vestment and the sense of importance it created; then a member of the youth group. These associations were especially vital to me after my father died, for his death meant that great insecurity entered my twelve-year-old life. As I was forced to deal somewhat prematurely with the responsibilities of the adult world, I found this church to be a very real anchor. It was a place where I was known and where I belonged. It was not long before it also provided me with a surrogate father.

In 1945 the old rector retired, and his replacement was different from any minister I had ever known. He was in his early thirties, happy-go-lucky and debonair. He wore white buck shoes (pretty stylish for that day!), and he drove a convertible, which was, of course, unheard of for a parson. His wife was a Georgia belle of exquisite beauty, who smoked cigarettes in a very worldly way using a golden cigarette holder. Suddenly, in this man, I had an ideal to follow, a hero to emulate. To be like Bob Crandall became the height of my ambition. He liked me, perhaps because I was the only acolyte who would serve at the 8 A.M. service. This he allowed me to do, despite the fact that I became nauseated, deathly ill, or fainted with great regularity. My padre had told me that the church insisted that one should always receive communion while fasting, which I was determined to do or die trying.

It never occurred to me to question my faith. God and Jesus intermingled for me. I never straightened out the resurrection or the ascension, and I did not really care. It only mattered that the church affirmed me, and affirm me it did. The only significant successes of my early life were church successes.

In my last year of high school, I took a class in Bible in the public school. That was still possible in America in the late forties. My teacher was a lovely "religious" woman. She did not wear make-up, for that was "against the teaching of the Bible," she said. She was a deeply devout gentle soul, genuinely admired but rabidly fundamentalist. To her the Bible was the word of God! Every word, every comma, God had dictated—and in the King James version, too! But how she did make those stories live! I was mesmerized with the tales of David, the adventures of Paul, and the story of the cross. She believed in "memory work," so I committed great chunks of scripture to memory, which made me a rare Episcopalian indeed. I was an avid student, and I began to read the Bible daily. I knew its content well. My teacher's pious, evangelistic approach was very revival-oriented in a Protestant direction. It featured making a decision for Jesus "as my personal Saviour." I learned gospel hymns like "Sweet Hour of Prayer," and I became known as the "religious" member of my high-school class. Frequently, I was called on to give the chapel devotional at our school assembly. My religion made me "somebody," though I still did not question its content. If God wanted Jonah to be in the belly of the whale for three days, that certainly was not any great problem for God, nor was it for me.

I went to college determined to prepare for the ministry. When the power of a great modern secular university suddenly challenged my life, I experienced my first faith crisis. My philosophy professor was an atheist. Another professor, I learned, had once been a Congregationalist minister but had resigned the ministry, repudiated his faith, and upon receiving his doctorate he entered the academic world as a teacher dedicated to destroying "superstitious religion." He bragged about his emancipation from the intellectual shackles of Christianity. It was under such experiences as these that my literal Bible exploded. My religious certainty evaporated. My sense of identity was challenged. I met this crisis by abandoning the authority of the literal scriptures and accepting the authority of a divine church. I became an anglo-catholic. I filled my life with religious disciplines and rules. I was moralistic beyond belief. There was no argument allowable beyond the words, "the church teaches." I found a group of like-minded people on the campus. All of us, I suspect, were deeply insecure people hiding from a great deal of reality. I zoomed through college with very high grades, completing my degree program in three years. But inwardly it was an intense struggle to preserve my faith and, beyond that, my sacred identity. This struggle demanded that I isolate my faith, build a fence around it, and refuse to question it. I paid that price, and with the direction of my life thus set, I entered graduate school to prepare for my priestly vocation.

Seminary was a relaxed environment for me because here there was a community of faith. No one shattered my inner creed. They shattered my naïveté, my intense moralism, my need for an authoritarian church of rigid discipline; but my faith remained intact. Here I learned the tradition, the history, "the faith," that I was to proclaim and defend. It was a very intellectual experience for me. My mind was at peace. My confidence returned. After three years I graduated and began to practice the calling for which I had yearned.

My first assignment was to a small church adjacent to the campus of Duke University in Durham, North Carolina. Armed with my new-found confidence, I proclaimed my intellectual Christ to that community with some success. I knew enough of the fundamentalistic heritage out of which so many students came that I could speak their language and offer them new possibilities. I stood somewhere between the religious heritage they had left and a complete abandonment of any religion. The post—World War II religious revival was still on. The reality of the atomic era was not yet fully digested. What I was able to offer seemed a popular midpoint. I clarified the science-religion conflict. I introduced the form criticism approach to Bible study. I delved into the psychological meanings of life and worship. Yet interestingly enough, I avoided the central issue. I never probed the Christ figure. He was the inviolate holy of holies for me.

My career in the ministry was the meteoric rise of the bright young man. After less than three years of "impressing" the university world, I moved to a grand old parish in eastern North Carolina. Then only twenty-six

years old, I knew my way around in the world of ecclesiastical politics and found myself, time after time, in the
right place at the right moment and able to do the right
thing. But that inner conviction, that very ground upon
which everything I did was finally based, grew weaker
and fuzzier with every passing day. These feelings I repressed while I delved into a new Sunday School curricu-
lum, group-life laboratories, and sensitivity training. I
worked hard on my sermons, and I presume it showed
for I developed some power of oratory that began to be
recognized. Invitations to speak in various places increased, and my orbit of travel became wider and wider. I
think I must have been like the minister who wrote on
the margin of his sermon, "Argument weak; yell like
hell!" I hid from the crises of my faith in the success of
my profession.

That success was deeply threatened in the late fifties
and early sixties by the racial conflict within my region.
But I discovered that social action could be an avenue for
escape from the torture of theological doubt. My deepest
and most honest convictions could be expressed politically
much more easily than theologically. It shocked me to admit that fact to myself, but it was nonetheless true.

It was in this internal wilderness that I first read John
Robinson's *Honest to God.* I was vacationing on the Outer
Banks of North Carolina. In my intellectual snobbery, I
did not consider it a great book at that time. The
thought it projected was not particularly new it quoted
Tillich, Bultmann, and Bonhoeffer, all of whom I had
previously read. But this book put together many of my
own doubts and questions. In effect, it "let the cat out of
the bag." It was no longer possible for me to play the
role of the believing parson with the same certainty.
Words and phrases became intolerable clichés that I could

no longer use. I am sure I read the book three times before I put it away that summer. Robinson gave me the courage to dare, to probe and to question openly. I have never been the same since. I was driven to my roots and forced to think again about everything I believed, about how I worshiped, and whether or not I could pray.[1] All of this went on inside me while I continued to preach each week, lead worship, bury the dead, counsel the troubled, and try to keep my life from breaking apart in all directions at once.

It was at this time that I moved to a large church in central Virginia. Once again it was close to an academic community, and it provided exactly what I needed for the searching my faith then required. I started a Sunday morning Bible class that met for an hour before worship each week. I determined that above all else, in this class I would be honest in my search for truth, and I would follow in whatever direction the quest for truth led me. The class became a community conversation piece. It was regularly described as scholarly, radical, iconoclastic, and with other adjectives that I dare not repeat. The fundamentalists departed to safer congregations, but the doubters began to come back to church. The class was so well attended that my critics dared not challenge it outright. I remember that when I did a special unit on the Virgin Birth, there was a standing room only crowd of people who gathered—including members of the press. It convinced me that the day had long since passed when Christian spokespersons should hedge their arguments or pull their punches so as not to offend the traditionally religious.

It is interesting that in that class I almost never roamed out of the Hebrew scriptures. The more I probed those scriptures, the more passionate grew my admiration for the Hebrew people. I regularly went on Friday night to the synagogue to worship, and I acquired the nickname "the blond rabbi of Lynchburg." I did not hide my enthusiasm for everything Jewish, nor my admiration for the nation of Israel and its people. I plunged into the prophets: Isaiah, Jeremiah, Hosea, Amos, Micah—these became intimate friends. I studied the Psalms, primarily to discover how they revealed the Hebrew attitude toward life. Here I discovered I could stand, live, and love. I became a Hebrewphile, and in this I found a point of view, a frame of reference that was real. What I believed and what I proclaimed were finally in harmony; and in that there was great freedom. Yet I never seemed quite able to get to the Jesus story of the Gospels. I simply contented myself with the fact that Jesus was a Hebrew, a child of this people whom I had come to admire so much, a product of the heritage that I was discovering. Occasionally there were questions, usually humorous questions, about when I would ever get to the Christian writings. The suggestion was even made that I never would, that I was afraid to, that I did not know enough about Christianity to teach it. These things were said in jest, but there was much truth in them. When, after four years, I finally agreed to begin a study of the gospels the following fall, I literally put myself on notice that the days of hiding were at an end.

I had planned to be in Tokyo for eight weeks that summer as priest-in-charge of an English-speaking church there. In that period I hoped to be able to do intensive study to prepare for that plunge. However, in May the trip to Tokyo was canceled, and in August I accepted a call to Richmond, Virginia. Probing the Jesus story was thus postponed, the faith crisis would not have to be faced—not quite yet. I brought the Bible class with me to my new congregation, but for the first three years, once again I confined myself to the Hebrew scriptures. With even greater zeal I went to depths I never dreamed of in the exploration of the faith of the Hebrews. I spent one entire year on nothing but the book of Genesis, living daily with the writings of Gerhard von Rad. At other times I touched the Christian writings, but only for specific subjects like the theology of Paul as expressed in Romans. (It is amazing how learned one can seem discussing the theology of Paul without committing oneself to much of anything!)

It was at this point that the luncheon conversation with my business friend took place, and I knew that the moment had come for me to dig in or to face some very serious problems. So I devoted that year to an exploration of the central issue of my faith: Who is Jesus of Nazareth? I was convinced that I must see Jesus in a Hebrew context. No other vantage point would hold reality for me. I entered this area with fear, for I was not at all certain of the outcome. The search, however, proved rewarding beyond measure.

I am not a systematic theologian, and to be one is not my goal. Rather, I could only hope to illumine from various angles this figure who stands at the center of all that the Christian Church is. I was determined not to be put off by the thought forms through which Jesus had been traditionally communicated; neither would I hold any words or creedal statements sacrosanct. I was prepared to reject anything I could not translate into the language of my secular world. I made Luke my primary teacher, with only occasional sorties into the writings of Mark, John, Matthew, or Paul.[2]

In this study I found a Lord, a center for my being. Behind the supernatural framework of the first century,

behind the language of myth, magic, and superstition, I
discovered a life I wanted to know; a life that possessed a
power I wanted to possess; a freedom, a wholeness for
which I had yearned for years. In my broken insecurity,
with my insatiable ego needs, I came to stand in awe of
this life. In any study, I first sought to be a cold and penetrating rationalist, seeking to pull back the layers of religious accretion that hid this Jesus from me; but somewhere in the process I discovered that I had become a
kind of Hebrew mystic, and my awe and my reverence
had been replaced by worship. Inside that worship, the titles *Saviour, Lord, Son of the Living God* became words I
now can say. The joy of that affirmation was more than
worth the tortuous process through which I had
journeyed.

I do not mean to suggest that I have arrived at some
mystical plateau where my search has ended, where
doubts are no more, or that I now possess some unearthly
peace of mind. Nothing could be further from the truth.
I have only arrived at a point where the search has a va-
lidity because I have tasted the reality of this presence, if
ever so slightly; and I know that even though I now see
through a glass darkly, I will soon see face to face.

2

❦

Learning to Think Biblically

I T W O U L D be the simple thing to plunge directly into the Jesus story, but I am convinced that this story cannot yet be heard. The cultural meanings that color and distort the traditional Christian language are too deep, too set, too familiar, and too unquestioned. Our quest must begin back in pre-Christian history where some new discoveries might assist in forcing new meanings into our holy words. Perhaps these discoveries might open doors to the Jesus story that will enable us to hear it in a fresh way.

In the Christian tradition, the words "religion" or "religious" are supposed to be full of positive connotations. It is a virtue to be religious. Religion is considered a valuable asset in the life of a community. Yet there are also some negative vibrations associated with those terms. When a person is described as a religious person, I, for one, feel a slight tremor of discomfort, a minus sign. The religious people that I have known have not been my favorite people. They are not the ones I would choose for friends. When I was a high-school student, those members of our class who were known as religious tended to be repressed, pious, even angry. Religion seemed to be a compensating factor for something that was missing from their "being," if you will.

In grief situations that I have entered as a pastor, it is inevitably the religious person who is insensitive, who feels compelled to speak surface assurances, who suppresses real feelings with homilies on faith, and who readily supplies pat answers for difficult and complex questions.

I must admit that since my early days as a member of the clergy I have reacted negatively to the designation of myself as a "religious" person. I did not want to look like "a preacher." Perhaps our culture's stereotype of the "person of the cloth" offends me. Whenever a member of the clergy is portrayed in movies, television, or the comics, he or she is invariably pompous, soft, and irrelevant; on the outside of life, looking in. The exceptions to this image are so unusual that they carry the whole drama just because they are unexpected. I think of Bing Crosby as the young and mischievous Roman Catholic priest in *Going My Way* or Burt Lancaster as *Elmer Gantry*. Neither do I want to sound like "a preacher." I deplore the stained-glass accents of my profession: the rigid tilt of voice and the pious innuendo, to say nothing of those canned religious phrases that show up time and again in the jargon of the trade. When Hollywood portrays a male religious voice, it seems as if the directors take a baritone and put his head in a barrel, so that his words have that round sound and heavenly echo.

It is striking to me that I do not think of Jesus the Christ in such religious categories. I find the word religion and the connotations of the word religious strangely absent from the biblical story. Nowhere in the gospel do I find the goal of Christian mission to be that of making one religious; rather, that goal is to set one free, to call one to life, to invite one to love. I have become so impressed with this contrast that the words biblical and religious have become for me not synonyms, but antonyms. I have repeatedly discovered that the traditional religious meanings of many of the words of our Christian heritage have moved so far afield from the biblical meaning the words had when they first entered our theological vocabulary that misunderstanding is impossible to avoid. I think of such words as spirit, faith, and salvation, for example. In order to begin the task of peeling back the layers that blind us to the beauty of the Christian story, we must start, I believe, by examining these words and the attitudes they convey, by comparing their traditional religious meaning with their original biblical meaning. In this process we will begin to develop "Hebrew eyes" through which to see our gospel.

The words spirit and soul are treasured words in the vocabulary of religion. The words are used synonymously. The things of the spirit are valued; the virtues of the soul are extolled. Indeed, the exhortations to be "spiritual" or to lead a "spirit-filled" life are abundant in almost every religious tradition. Much of the great devotional literature of the ages carries such exhortations. Spirituality is a blessing, we are told. Those of us who do not honestly feel spiritual either learn to fake it or to feel judged and inadequate.

An example of this occurred during my last year in seminary, as we were preparing for our canonical examinations. In my generation all candidates for the priesthood had to pass these examinations in their home diocese at the hands of the diocesan examining chaplains before they could be ordained. One of these examiners assigned us a book entitled *The Elements of the Spiritual Life* by F. P. Harton. We were to "read, mark, learn, and inwardly digest" it. It was undoubtedly the worst book I have ever read! It catalogued sins in a most legalistic way. It gave helpful hints on how to "let flesh retire, let sense be dumb." It prescribed specific directions on exactly how we could mortify our bodies and cultivate our souls, as if the two were diametrically opposed. I was twenty-four years old, proud of my lovely wife and beautiful six-month-old daughter, full of life and fun, and somehow "mortifying the body" was the last thing that seemed relevant to me. But read it, learn it, pass the exam on it— and forget it, I did.

Yet that book defines "spiritual" as our traditional religious language has come to think of it: pious, detached, given to contemplation, life-denying, and otherworldly. It brings to mind the image of folded hands and eyes cast heavenward. It has a feeling of softness about it. When clergypersons are described as spiritual, that tends to mean that they have a gaunt and hungry look. (Who ever heard of a spiritual fat person?) When a pulpit committee looking for a new minister states that "what this church needs is a spiritual priest," I hear them really saying that they want someone noncontroversial who will not be actively involved in efforts to change the world, confining his or her action only to praying for peace and justice. Indeed, I have discovered that the more conservative a congregation is, the more that congregation tends to want a spiritual pastor.

Yet the connotations we attribute to these words are nowhere near what spirit or spiritual mean in the biblical narrative. Our English words *soul* or *spirit* are our attempts to translate the Greek word *psyche* into English. In Greek *psyche* means the mind or the spirit; that is, the nonphysical aspect of our being. It is the word from which we get psychology, psychopathic, psychiatrist, etc. However, Christianity was not born in a Greek world, but in a Hebrew world. The Greek language was a resting place between the Hebrew original and our contemporary languages. Behind the Greek word *psyche*, we find two Hebrew words, *nephesh* and *ruach;* and by no stretch of the imagination did these Hebrew words mean the nonphysical aspect of our being. Indeed, had we translated *nephesh* and *ruach* directly into English, it is quite obvious that our words *soul* or *spirit* would be very inadequate vehicles to carry their meanings. Only the intermediate way station of the Greek language has in it the traditional connotations we read into our words.

Nephesh literally means "breath"—more particularly, the "breath of God." *Ruach* literally means "wind"—the "wind of God." The primary purpose of breath and wind was to animate, to make vital, to bring alive the whole person, body and mind. In a Hebrew or biblical context, to be spiritual was to be animated, vital, alive physically, which is quite different from its traditional religious meaning.[1]

In the Yahwist[2] writer's story of creation (Gen. 2:4ff), which is approximately four hundred years earlier than the more familiar seven-day account of the priestly[3] writer (Gen. 1:1–2:4), we find a rather anthropomorphic God who created a human body by molding it out of the dust of the earth, much as we might make a mud pie. But that body was dead, inert, until God breathed *nephesh* into it, and only then did it come alive. To be indwelt by the spirit, the breath of God, was not to be pious but to be alive, to be vital. The sign of the presence of the spirit was the presence of life. The function of spirit was to bring life. How different! How fresh! Again and again in

the biblical story we find this insight confirmed. When
Elijah's spirit rested on Elisha, the result was the coming
to full power, to live and be for Elisha.

In 597 B.C.E., Jerusalem fell to the Babylonians, and
the Hebrew people were carried off into exile. Among
those who joined the long march to captivity was a priest
named Ezekiel, whose prophetic career was pivotal in the
history of Judah. Ezekiel had a vivid imagination. He constantly had dreams and visions of exaggerated proportions
and always in color. He knew that his nation was pros-
trate, his holy city occupied, his temple defiled, his people
in captivity. Judah's future seemed bleak; this was a dead
nation. So Ezekiel had a dream. In this dream he saw a
valley, in which there was nothing but dead, dry bones—a
symbol of Judah. The voice of the Lord said, "Ezekiel,
can these bones live again?" Ezekiel answered, "Lord,
only you know that."

Then the Lord caused the *ruach*—the life-giving wind,
God's spirit—to blow over that valley. There was a shak-
ing, rattling, and rolling of bones the likes of which no vision has since produced. And that which had been dead
was brought to life by the wind, the *ruach,* the spirit of
God blowing over it. When the people of Judah responded to the spirit of God, the result was not that they became pious or religious, but that they became alive.
Wherever one meets spirit biblically, it is announced by
the presence of life.

In the book of Acts, Luke portrays the disciples as
waiting in the upper room for the empowerment they
had been promised. Despite the resurrection, they were
fearful, still in hiding, not yet in possession of their life.
Then, says Luke, there came a mighty rushing wind—
God's *ruach*—with tongues of fire, and they were filled
with the spirit! They became self-possessed people, free of

fear, alive to God and to each other. With the power and energy of whole people, they took on the world and turned it upside down for their Lord. The Holy Spirit came at Pentecost and gave them life—life that was to become the light of the world. That is the function of spirit, biblically: to give life.

We still have echoes of the biblical meaning of the word *spirit* in our language, but somehow we never seem to hear them when we are thinking theologically. We refer to a "spirited horse," alive and vital, as opposed to a "dispirited nag," swayback and inert. We hear of a "spirited address" or a "spirited debate," which means lively and animated, not tedious and boring. We refer to good Scotch whisky as a "spirited beverage," by which we mean that it has punch and power that we fail to respect at our own risk. Our young people, under the influence of the music of black America, now talk of "soul music"; that is, music into which the whole of life is thrown— mind, body, and spirit; music that has the beat of a heart throbbing with life and emotion. Appropriately, the word *soul* was chosen to describe it.

Biblically then the function of the spirit is to make vital, to call into being, to free, to make whole, to establish community based on life. To be spiritual means to be alive. To be filled with the spirit means to be free to live. It does not mean to be turned toward the nonphysical, to be pious, to cultivate the virtues of the soul. Yet this has become its religious meaning. I yearn to be spiritual in the biblical sense. I am not at all eager to be spiritual in a religious sense.

The second word to consider is *faith*. Faith has an immense cash value in the vocabulary of religion. When the clergy can think of nothing else to say in critical situations, they retreat behind the word faith: "You just have

to have faith," they say. To have faith is to believe even
where there is no evidence to support that belief. Beyond
the aid of reason or evidence, there is that gap over
which we leap with the fiberglass pole of "faith." Essen-
tially in our religious jargon, faith is an activity of the
mind that has to do with the act of believing as opposed
to doubting. If faith is present, then doubt is banished or
at least papered over. What we cannot understand, religious people assure us, we must accept on faith, with a
mighty effort at repression of whatever makes believing
difficult. Faith is something we are not encouraged to
question, lest it crumble and we are rendered desolate.

But biblical faith is not an act of the mind or of the
intellect at all. If the Hebrews had located faith in an organ of the body, it would have been in the heart. For
faith to the Hebrew was not a matter of belief; rather, it
was a matter of an attitude toward life. Biblically, the person of faith was the person of courage who dared to venture into life.

For the biblical mind, God was always revealed in life,
in history. God was always calling people into tomorrow.
If people wanted to find God, they turned toward life,
and stepped boldly into the future. The capacity to enter
life, to confront the unknown, to venture forward, to find
affirmation for one's own being: this was to have faith. So
the author of the Epistle to the Hebrews could say, "By
faith Abraham went out from Ur of the Chaldees to form
a new people." By faith Moses left the security of Egypt
for the insecurity of the wilderness, confident only that
God was in that wilderness and that God would be revealed there. Faith for the Hebrews meant being open to
God at work in the world and boldly stepping into life to
meet God.

Again the seeds of distortion are seen in the translation from Hebrew to Greek to English. Our word faith translates the Greek word *pistis,* from which we get epistemology (the study of knowledge). In Greek *pistis* was clearly a property and function of the mind. It was easy to identify faith with "pious belief" or "religious opinion." But behind that Greek word *pistis* was a Hebrew word, *emunah,* which meant the capacity to trust, the courage to act, the willingness to commit. The biblical mind believed that God was made known in history. This was called "revelation." Faith was the courageous openness to life that enabled the Hebrew to discern the presence of God in history. Hebrew faith had room in it for intellectual doubt: "Lord, I believe, help thou my unbelief" (Mark 9:24); for faith was not an activity of the mind; rather, it was of the whole person. It dealt with *being* far more than it dealt with *doing.* A man or woman of faith, biblically, would rise from their bed in the morning, prepare to engage their world, open themselves to perceive the depth dimensions of life, and live in courageous expectation that God was present in life, calling them to live and to be. This faith accompanied the Hebrews through the wilderness to their promised land. It made them capable as a nation of surviving the Babylonian captivity. It brought them back generations later to rebuild their homeland. It enabled them to live without a home for two thousand years and still not lose their identity. God was in life for this people; to meet God, one had to live.

Religiously, to have faith is to believe properly, without doubt. Biblically, to have faith is to enter life with the courageous expectation that the more deeply one lives, the more deeply one will experience the God who is revealed in life. There is quite a difference. One wonders how many of those who believe themselves to be without

faith in the religious sense might discover themselves to
be giants of faith in the biblical sense!

Finally, we examine the word *salvation*. Religiously,
this word has come to mean to be "lifted out of life."
The old gospel hymns of the nineteenth century exhorted
the Lord to "plant our feet on higher ground," and they
extolled the love that "lifted me" when "I was sinking
deep in sin." Salvation was defined in the Middle Ages as
the "beatific vision"; that is, the end of the Christian life
was to be lifted out of and beyond the world. An Aquinas
poem, sung to a plainsong setting, says: "That thy face
unveiled, I at last may see, with the blissful vision, blest
my God of thee." The life of contemplation was designed
to escape the changes and chances of mortal life and to
achieve peace, tranquility, a taste of heaven. Salvation was
deliverance from the world.

Some who read this will consider it a dated comment,
for the church in recent decades has been a very alive,
daring, socially aware institution. But those of us who
serve specific congregations of real people know the price
that has been paid for this stance of involvement. We
have seen the incredible resistance with which Christian
social action has been met by the traditionally religious
people who are quite convinced that the Christian Church
has no business being involved with anything other than
religion, God, salvation, and heaven. They are certain
that any other focus is wrong. If salvation is "deliverance
from this world," as it has come to be in religious language for years, then these critics of recent church activities are accurate. But nowhere in the biblical story can
such a view of salvation be garnered except by the most
violent and absurd wrenching of the text with precon-
ceived ideas. When traditionally religious people, who
happen quite often to be politically reactionary, urge their

ministers to "stick to the Bible," it is quite obvious to me that they have never read the Bible, or at least they have never listened to what they were reading, for they are in fact urging them to stick to the most revolutionary book in western civilization.

It is sometimes amusing to watch a conservative, traditional congregation come together for the typical Christmas pageant that they always think is so beautiful and so sweet. The angel announces to Mary that she is to bear the Christ child, and then Mary—usually a lovely young girl with a lilting voice—steps out and sings Mary's song, called "The Magnificat." She sings of this Christ that she will produce and of his mission. He will "put down the mighty from their seats." It is a line that sounds like a call to revolution. He will "exalt the humble and meek," she continues; words that sound like a call for a classless society. "He hath filled the hungry with good things and the rich he hath sent empty away." These words seem to contain no less than a proposal to redistribute the wealth.

Pious, otherworldly platitudes are found in neither the stance nor the attitude of the Bible. This book, with its thin, gold-edged pages, that people think is the story of otherworldly salvation, is in fact a story about power— real earthly power—power that could change lives, disrupt traditions, overturn customs. It was not a Sunday School tea party that took on, conquered, converted, and transformed the Roman Empire; this transformation was a very worldly performance. Salvation, biblically, is not an escape from life; it is a filling full of life.

The Bible is a book that scores idolatry on every page, but it defines idolatry as any worship that is not related to life. It is a book that proclaims that if one professes to love God but does not love one's neighbor, that person is a liar. It is a book that insists, in a paraphrase of the words of Amos, that true worship is only the justice among people being offered to God; and human justice is nothing but the worship of God being acted out. To be more specific, in the words of Jesus, the test of the Christian life that will be applied at the moment of judgment is not how religious have you been or how involved have you been in church activities, but how sensitive have you been to human need. "When I was hungry, did you feed me? When I was naked, did you clothe me? When I was in prison, did you visit me? Inasmuch as you have done it unto one of the least of these, you did it unto me" (Matt. 25:31ff).

The Bible is a worldly, uncomfortable, disturbing, non-complacent book that somehow men and women have come to hear as a religious, comfortable, otherworldly volume. The Bible is life-centered, not heaven-centered. It begins with the account of creation, and that creation—including physical reality, matter, bodies, this world—is pronounced "good." It is oriented toward life, not away from it. Underlying the Scriptures, there is an inescapable attitude of joy in creation and appreciation and love for life.

Nowhere is this better seen than in the Yahwist's version of the creation story (Gen. 2:4ff), but one must scratch beneath the prim and proper cadences of the King James Bible to find it. In that story God had created and "enlivened" man—Adam—who lived in the Garden of Eden in solitary splendor. But Adam was lonely, so he asked God to make him a friend. The Lord responded to this request and fashioned, say, a polar bear, which he brought before Adam. "That's a very nice polar bear, Lord, but that's not exactly what I had in mind," Adam responded. So God tried again, making a cat, a dog, a lion, a tiger, a giraffe, and brought each in turn before

Adam, who named[4] them yet continued to express dissatisfaction. In this way, said the Yahwist writer, all the animals of the world were created. As nice as the animals were, they just did not fill the need, the sense of incompleteness that caused Adam to request a friend in the first place. Finally, one gets the impression that God was a little impatient with Adam. Nothing seemed to please him, but the Lord decided to try one more time. He put Adam to sleep, and, in the words of the spiritual, "he took a rib from Adam's side and made Miss Eve for to be his bride." He placed Eve, with all the grace and charm of her feminine lines, in front of Adam and then gently awakened him. Adam sat up, and you get the impression that his eyes popped out of his head a few inches as he sought to embrace visually this incredibly beautiful creature before him. The King James Bible recorded that Adam said, "This is now bone of my bones and flesh of my flesh. She shall be called woman, because she was taken out of man" (Gen. 2:23). But that is not exactly what the text said in Hebrew. In Hebrew, a slang expression was used to express excitement, happiness, anticipation. It might better be translated: "Hot diggity, Lord, you finally did it!" There was life-affirming joy in the biblical attitude toward the world. Life was good to the Hebrew, for God made it so.

The same attitude springs forth in the story of Moses' death, as recorded in the book of Deuteronomy (34:7). Moses had been a man of overwhelming dominance in the life of this Hebrew nation. His achievements were too numerous to count. He had established this people, led them out of slavery, through the Red Sea,[5] and into the wilderness. He had overseen the formulation of a covenant relationship with their God. He was viewed as the giver of the Law and the Ten Commandments. He had brought

them to the threshold of their promised land with its
dreams of milk and honey. But here he died. The Hebrew people wanted to eulogize Moses, to carve in stone,
as it were, appropriate words to praise him. Out of all his
accomplishments, what did they elect to say? The King
James version states: "And Moses was an hundred and
twenty years old when he died: his eye was not dim, nor
his natural force abated" (Deut. 34:7). But again that was
not exactly what the Hebrew text said. The lusty, life-
loving Hebrews surveyed Moses' achievements and then
singled out the highest praise they could heap upon their
hero. They said, "Moses died at age one hundred twenty,
and even at that age he was a virile, potent male." To
the Hebrews, that was admirable beyond anything else.

I remember discussing this worldly aspect of our
Christian heritage one day with a young, rigid, life-
denying, otherworldly clergyman of a very fundamentalistic tradition. He was a perfect stereotype: About six feet
tall but weighing only one hundred and thirty pounds, he
was dressed in a black suit, a white shirt, a thin black tie,
black shoes, and white socks. His voice had a holy sound.
Not surprisingly, he found it very difficult to comprehend
or appreciate my point of view as I extolled the life that I
found affirmed in the biblical story. In a graceful way,
trying to salvage some area of agreement as we parted, he
pronounced the familiar cliché, "Well, Jack, I guess it
doesn't matter that we don't agree on everything, especially as we know we are both Christians traveling toward
the same final destination." "You're right, Jim," I answered, "but the difference is that I'm enjoying the trip a
heck of a lot more than you are!"

I think that is biblical. God's creation is to be loved,
the world is to be entered, life is to be lived. Salvation is

to make life whole and free, sensitive to the selves we are, the neighbor we love, and the God we worship. In this attitude I find a clue to the understanding of the Bible. It focuses on the here and now, it calls us to step out and embrace the future by affirming the present. It insists that God is found in life; but once found there, it forces us to recognize that God is more than life, God is the transcendent source of life. The Hebrews had a vital concept of history. It was history that was moving toward a final and eternal destiny. History was the arena in which, and through which, the God Yahweh was revealed to the people and in which God called them into life. Because of this sense of history, the Hebrews produced prophets. These prophets were not fortune tellers or predictors of the future; rather, they were the ones who interpreted the revelation of God in the present events of history. They were concerned with life now, not with some otherworldly salvation.

Salvation, in its traditional religious definition, means "being saved; guaranteed heaven; the event beyond life." But biblically, salvation means "the fullness of living now as well as eternally." Eternity had little reality for the Hebrew, except insofar as it was received in the *now* of their lives.

Everywhere we look we find a vast chasm between traditional religious meanings and original biblical meanings in the language of our worship. Religion itself has come to be an activity having to do with sacred things, words, and places. But biblical thinking has little or nothing to do with such a view of religion.

The Hebrews were the most God-intoxicated people the world has ever known, but they were never a religious people in our sense of the word. It is difficult to find in the Hebrew scriptures a pious, otherworldly Hebrew. Very few can be located in history, the possible exception being the Hasidim. Rather, the Hebrews were life-centered, life-affirming, life-loving people who worshiped the God of life, creation, and history. They found joy in life. Religion has tended to repress joy. Hebrew worship celebrated the God of life. Contemporary religious worshipers seem to feel that joy or laughter is inappropriate in worship. If you have ever watched my fellow Episcopalians return from the altar after receiving communion, you would think that they had just lost their last friend or had just eaten a sour persimmon. Yet in that tradition they still refer to that service as a "celebration" of The Holy Eucharist.

The stained glass of many of our churches shuts out God's world with "heavenly" art. The organ music creates a pious mood with otherworldly sounds. The Elizabethan accents in our rituals say that worship is unreal. It must have a voice of the past, for it is not a part of the present.

Somehow in our history, biblical spirituality was replaced by religious spirituality, biblical faith by religious faith, biblical salvation by religious salvation, a biblical attitude toward life by a religious attitude toward life. Yet we live in a period of history in which nonreligious, secularized modern men and women are deeply concerned with these very biblical things: living life to its fullest, walking openly into the world, transforming the future, finding a transcendent meaning in the here and now. These same modern inhabitants of our secular world are convinced that Christianity does not support them in this quest, at least not the Christianity that emanates from the traditional Christian churches. The Jesus story is so overlaid with an otherworldly aura that he is not an attractive, appealing figure to them. How sad! How very sad!

So we begin to draw back the curtains. I hope hints of joyful excitement are beginning to fall, but the confusion is so deep that the restoration will not be easy. We look next at history to bring that confusion into better focus.

3

❦

The Transition into Religion

I A M a Hebrewphile. No people on the face of the earth do I admire the way that I admire the Hebrews. I would love to discover somewhere in my ancestry that I was the recipient of Jewish blood. I can easily understand why Adolf Hitler made them the victims of his persecution. He was determined to prove his master-race theories on behalf of the Aryan people. As long as the Jewish people existed, no claim of superiority on the part of any other national group could be unchallenged. My prejudice in the Hebrews' favor is inordinate because only after I got inside the Hebrew mind did I perceive the meaning of both my world and my Christ.

I am convinced that if the Bible is going to be understood in our day, we must develop "Hebrew eyes" and "Hebrew attitudes" toward life. The Bible is a Hebrew book, telling the story of the Hebrew people. Jesus was a Hebrew Lord. We, on the other hand, are Western people sharing a very diverse and sometimes contradictory heritage that comes from many sources. We have been shaped to some major degree by the Hebrew scriptures:

the sacredness of individual life and the sense of progress in history, for instance, are part of our common Hebrew inheritance. But we have also been molded and formed by the philosophical culture of ancient Greece, especially its dominant platonic and neoplatonic traditions. These two strands of our heritage, the Hebrew and the Greek, are not easily harmonized, for they have some very basic incompatibilities that give our history both a tension and a dynamism.

One might normally be led to expect that the religious part of our western world was shaped by our Hebrew background; and that the secular, modern mood of our day represented the gift of the worldly Greeks. Strangely enough, I think that the exact opposite is the case. When I analyze the language, the concepts, the understandings, the meanings in the traditional religious patterns today, I discover that they come to us not from our biblical Hebrew heritage at all; rather, they are the direct outgrowth of the neoplatonic roots of Greek philosophy. To compound the paradox, it is my contention that the peculiarly modern attitude—worldly, nonreligious, scientifically oriented—is far more Hebraic and biblical than the modern mind dares to imagine.

How did this strange contrast come about? How did Christian people who acknowledge a first-century Hebrew man to be their Lord come to express their faith in the religious categories of the Greek mind? How is it that those who think of themselves as nonreligious, secular people also think quite biblically, quite Hebraically? Let us look at our roots.

If I could draw a picture that would adequately depict for me a Hebrew view of reality, I would draw two circles: a smaller one within the larger one. The smaller circle I would name *the world;* the larger circle I would name

God (Fig. 1). To the Hebrew, God and the world were
not antithetical, nor were they identical. God was the creator; the world was the creature. God was bigger than the
creation, but the creation revealed the creator's glory.
The Hebrew creation story affirmed the goodness of life.
It was creation ex nihilo; that is, God was totally responsible for the material physical stuff of life.[1] God made it
all, and when it was complete God surveyed it and pronounced it good indeed. The physical world was the object of God's love. It was showered with God's blessings:
sunshine and rainfall. For human life a garden was built
called Eden. God walked in the garden "in the cool of
the evening" (Gen. 3:8). Material things were good; they
were meant to be used. Physical things were good; they
were meant to be appreciated. Life was good; it was
meant to be lived. The world was good; it was the object

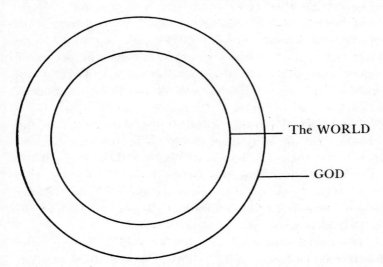

The WORLD

GOD

Fig. 1   THE HEBREW BIBLICAL VIEW

of the divine love, and was therefore meant to be engaged. With great joy the Hebrews could sing of God's world and of God's creation.

So, as we noted previously, to be spiritual, for the Hebrews, meant to be alive to God and alive to the world. It did not mean to be pious or otherworldly. To have faith, for the Hebrew, was to have the courage to enter life, for that is where God is to be found, always calling us into tomorrow. History was the arena of God's revelation, and figures of history—even those like Cyrus, who did not know it—were the agents of the divine purposes. The Hebrew prophets were those who could perceive the meaning of the present moment of time and interpret from it the purpose of God in history.

When the early Hebrews thought about the "good" person, they did not envision the "religious" person, at least not until after the exile, when pharisaism flourished.[2] Rather, their image of the "good" person was the whole person, the free person, the realized person. They never divided human life into component parts of body, mind, and spirit with different activities appropriate only to the different components.

The Hebrews were so busy living life here in the world that they thought very little about life after death. This is not to say that they did not believe in life after death, but only that they did not pay much attention to it. When the Hebrews did think about life beyond death, however, it was in terms of the continuing life of the whole person, not the continued existence of merely one aspect of the human life such as the nonphysical soul, for example. Immortality of the soul is not a biblical concept. Indeed, there is no word in the Hebrew language that means what the Greek word *psyche* meant or what we, translating from the Greek, tend to mean by the word soul in English.

This is our biblical heritage, our Hebrew background, out of which our Christian faith was born. This is the attitudinal context of our Lord. The story of Jesus of Nazareth is the story of the God who so loved the world that God was made known in it and through it as an historic person (John 3:16). The Hebrew Jesus of Nazareth is the one who said: "I have come that you might have life and have it abundantly" (John 10:10). He is also the one who charged his disciples to go into all the world to reveal discipleship through love. The Christian story asserts that if one wants to look for God, one must look at life, at history, and at the world.

Jesus was a specific figure of history. He was born about 4 B.C.E. at Bethlehem.[3] He lived in a particular town, Nazareth. He taught in historic cities: Capernaum, Bethsaida, Gersa. He died during the administration of an historic procurator, whose name was Pontius Pilate, about 30 C.E. at Jerusalem. The biblical God must be sought in life, in history. That is the specific message of the gospel account, a gospel born in a Hebrew world.

However, there was in the ancient world another way of perceiving life that contrasted sharply with the Hebrew view that in time would both counter and overwhelm the Hebrew attitude. This view reached its classic definitive form in the philosophical mind of Greece, though it obviously had much earlier antecedents.[4] Underlying the Greek view was a very basic dualism that contradicted the Hebrew understanding of the relationship between God and the world. If I had to depict dualism symbolically, it would look like the circles in Figure 2. There was in the dualistic mind of Greek philosophy a separation between the spiritual and the physical, between God and the

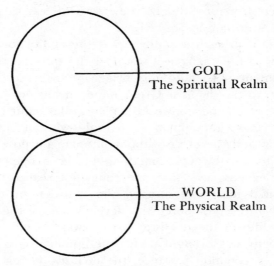

GOD
The Spiritual Realm

WORLD
The Physical Realm

Fig. 2 THE DUALISTIC VIEW

world. There was no clearly defined doctrine of creation underlying the dualism; rather, there were two eternal realities: spirit and matter. They were in the beginning and always would be. In this view of the shape of reality, if you wanted to meet God you would not turn toward the world but away from it; you would not become involved in life but would rather retreat from it. God, to the Greek mind, was not revealed in the events of history but in the mental discipline of contemplation. God was not a force with which to reckon but an idea on which to meditate. The more timeless or changeless anything was in this dualistic interpretation, the more spiritual (good) it was. Thus, goodness was better seen in forms, ideals, ideas. Physical things that were concrete and specific were more given to the world of change and decay and were, therefore, closely identified with the world of physical

matter. Correspondingly, they were of less value and, finally, were considered evil.

Faith, in such a context, was the ability to make contact with the changeless world of the spiritual realm, with
the intellect; so faith was primarily an act of the mind.
Spirit, to the dualistic Greek mind, meant not life but the
nonphysical, the nonworldly, piety. Like nature, time and
history were thought of as cyclical—without beginning or
ending and therefore without ultimate purpose.

Life, finally, was something to be escaped. Certainly
the idea was clear that one could not realize the human
potential until one escaped the "burden of the flesh,"
which forever hindered the development of the soul. The
good life, in the dualistic system, was the life where the
evil body was brought under the domination of the good
soul. In common parlance, the dualistic Greek tended to
divide life somewhere about the diaphragm. Below the
diaphragm was the seat of physical, carnal passion and desire, which must be harnessed and controlled. Above the
diaphragm was the center of thought, intellect, ideas, the
ability to grasp beauty, truth, goodness, and God. So it
made sense to talk about the spiritual exercise of mortifying the flesh and to exhort one to climb the ladder of
spiritual awareness and sensitivity.

It is easy to understand that when the dualistic mind
of ancient Greece thought about life after death, it was
always in terms of the immortality of the soul. The soul,
pure spirit, was incarcerated in the flesh, and death was
the moment of escape. The body returned to the earth to
participate in the changing, decaying process of physical
matter. The soul soared heavenward to the eternal spirit
realm, free at last of its fleshly burden.

The Christian faith was born in a Hebrew context,
serving a Hebrew Lord—a life-giving, life-loving, whole,

free man. But when this faith moved outward from the Hebrew world into the Mediterranean civilization, it inevitably confronted the dualistic mind of the Greek world. After that confrontation, Christianity was never the same, for there was no escape from the necessity of translating Christian thought into dualistic categories.

From the events of Good Friday and Easter, which we can date at approximately 30 C.E., to the historic battle of Milvian Bridge in 312 C.E., the Christian movement had been constantly under duress from its hostile world. The air of persecution was always pervasive, even if the actual heat of persecution was not always intense. Because of this, Christian thought in the first three hundred years of its life was much more polemical than it was systematic. It expressed the battle of life and death between the church and the world. The world, however, meant the geopolitical world of a hostile power—the Roman Empire—and not the world of God's creation. Then came the decisive battle at Milvian Bridge, Constantine's victory, and the resultant Edict of Milan in 313 made Christianity a legal religion within the Empire.

Suddenly, the world was no longer the enemy. However, thought forms do not change easily. For three hundred years the Christian story had been proclaimed over against a hostile world, and its teaching assumed this enemy force. Its energies were always girded for battle. Now a vacuum was created where once the enemy had been.

In response to this circumstance, Christian people did a very interesting thing. Perhaps unconsciously, without quite perceiving what was occurring, the place of the enemy world was taken over by the physical realm of the dualistic mind. Previously it had been "church versus world" in the thought process of Christians, and now it became "church versus worldliness" (Fig. 3). As Christian

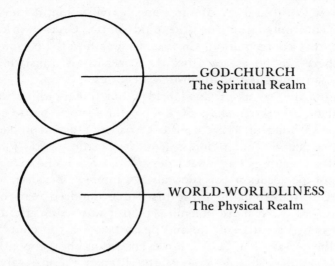

GOD-CHURCH
The Spiritual Realm

WORLD-WORLDLINESS
The Physical Realm

Fig. 3   The Christian Identification with Dualism

leaders began to talk of adopting creeds, clarifying doctrine, establishing worship free of persecution, they
thought more and more in terms of the underlying dualistic mind-set and attitudes of the Greek world. Dualism became the basic mental assumption through which the
Christian faith was viewed.

It was a gradual occurrence. All material things did
not suddenly become evil; it was much more subtle than
that. First, value systems arose in which the more spiritual
otherworldly activities achieved a higher status than the
more fleshly worldly activities. This, however, became
simply a resting place in the inevitable descent into a
Christian dualism in which Christianity and the church
were identified with the realm of the spirit, and all world-

ly pursuits and physical concerns were identified with the
realm of the physical. Slowly but surely the Hebrew view
of the goodness of creation and the wholeness of life
were forgotten, and Christianity bought Greek dualism,
the inevitable result being what I now call the "Grecianization of the Gospel."

The historic signs of this were overwhelming. Soon
after the legalization of Christianity within the Empire by
Constantine, we witness the rise of the monastic movement in Christendom. The world became a place to be escaped, not to be engaged. Christians who followed the
"higher calling" turned their backs on life and gave
themselves to the "spiritual" pursuits of prayer, meditation, contemplation. They mortified the flesh, tortured
and denied their bodies in order to purge their souls of
the stains of evil.

Soon the spiritualization of the Blessed Virgin Mary
was in full swing. Mary became "perpetually virgin." She
could not bear children because in a dualistic world view,
the human body and its functions, especially sexual ones,
became evil. Mary had to be preserved from that evil, for
the womb that bore the Christ could not be defiled, a
point of view the Hebrews could never have entertained.
Perpetual virginity was proclaimed and all the brothers
and sisters of Jesus became "cousins" or children by
Joseph's previous marriage or something equally as farfetched. Before this attitude had run its course, Mary was
not only perpetually virgin, she was immaculately conceived and bodily assumed. In every possible way Mary's
contact with the evil physical realm of bodies was
removed.

This reasoning was carried on into the life of the
world. Marriage was for the spiritually weak. Certainly
those who sought ordination could not indulge the flesh,

so a celibate priesthood, denying the "evil desires" of the body, emerged and became in time the rule of the church. I look with some amusement on the story of Jesus healing Peter's mother-in-law in the Gospel of Mark (1:30–31). Peter was, according to tradition, the first pope, and one does not have a mother-in-law without marriage. So what was apparently good for the first pope became evil for subsequent popes, because Christianity had moved from a Hebrew attitude toward life to a dualistic Greek attitude.

The great Christological debates of the ecumenical councils of the fourth, fifth, and sixth centuries assumed the dualism of their world, and the mutually exclusive categories of divinity and humanity became the two poles of the irreconcilable conflict. How to maintain the divinity and the humanity of Jesus simultaneously was a problem of immense proportions in such a world. Every attempt at definition erred on one side or the other. One could not think at this time except in the categories of that world. Hence theological language inevitably reflected the underlying dualistic assumptions, which were nonbiblical.

Once the dualistic identification was made following the Edict of Milan in 313, the Grecianizing process in the church was speeded up. It was as if someone had placed a gigantic vacuum cleaner on the Hebrew view of reality and sucked all the goodness out of the world, all the wonder, the glory, the divinity of life—all the holiness, all the presence of God—and isolated these over against the world in a realm called "spiritual," leaving only the base, the physical, the material, the evil as the domain of the world. The dynamic forward thrust went out of life, and stagnation was the result. The goal of the Christian life was now not the transformation of the world but the beatific vision. Otherworldly concerns became dominant. This attitude reached its culmination, its high-water mark, in the thirteenth century. (To symbolize in diagram the way this concept looked in the Christian world in the thirteenth century, see Figure 4.)

As the church grew in dominance, the realm of the spirit with which the church had made its special identification grew in importance, while the realm of the physical began to shrink as an object of concern. By the thirteenth century, heaven was real, earth was transitory, passing, changing; and therefore something to be endured. The nineteenth-century hymn, "I'm but a stranger here, heaven is my home," could have been their theme song. In such a world no passion for life was exhibited, no war against injustice was fought, no reform movements were initiated. This world was considered too unimportant to be worthy of serious efforts at change, for it was

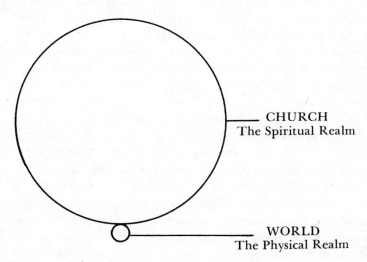

CHURCH
The Spiritual Realm

WORLD
The Physical Realm

Fig. 4   THE 13TH CENTURY

but a vale of tears, a place of sojourn in which to prepare for one's eternal destiny. There was a sanctified mood of resignation, of acceptance of one's status or circumstances, because life here did not really matter that much.

This fact has had its ramifications in our later history. Because efforts to reform life in this world, to increase justice among men and women, to throw off the shackles of human bondage were not the concern of Christians, they inevitably had to become the concern of non-Christians. This spiritualized, benign neglect by the church of the festering sores of injustice guaranteed that reform movements in western civilization would be violently anti-Christian movements. One has only to look at the French Revolution, the Russian Revolution, the Spanish Revolution to see on which side the institutional church took its stand. It was the pious, otherworldly attitude in the face of overt oppression and injustice that caused Karl Marx to utter his famous words that "religion is the opium of the people." The Grecianized, spiritual, otherworldly Christianity offered "pie in the sky, by and by, when you die." It drugged the populace into tolerating intolerable circumstances—"to do my duty in that state of life unto which it shall please God to call me" (Book of Common Prayer, p. 580). This viewpoint created the inert life, an accept-whatever-is attitude.

If the realm of the spirit was good and the realm of the material was evil, then to spend one's life investigating material reality was not only a waste of time but a positive evil. That time could better be spent developing the virtues of the soul. Hence there was in the thirteenth century little concern for science and an active discouragement of the scientific enterprise. Thus when the scientific pursuits did emerge in western civilization, they were inevitably anti-Christian and anti-religious. The science-versus-religion battle of the recent past was unavoidable given the antiworld, antiphysical reality stance of thirteenth-century Grecianized Christianity.

Since the soul was good and all-important, and the body was evil and unimportant, there was in the medieval period a low priority placed on the practice of medicine. Medicine's purpose of prolonging life simply delayed the moment when one escaped the unreal world for the bliss of heaven. The status of medical doctors in the thirteenth century was very low. They were body mechanics who plied their trade in a world that thought: "Why tarry here when so great a home as heaven awaits us?" Basically the practice of medicine was to relieve pain, not to prolong life. Status, in that day, was possessed by the clergy, who supposedly held in their hands the keys to eternal destiny; hence the title "doctor" was exclusively the title of the theologically learned.

To be a Christian in the thirteenth century, one turned away from life, turned away from the world, in order to seek contact with the transcendent, otherworldly power of the spirit. The more completely one could do that, the higher the status. There were levels of Christians: the monastics were the highest level, living under the vows of poverty, chastity, obedience, a life of total denial of "the world, the flesh, the devil." The secular clergy were next—celibate, at least in theory, though not living in monastic communities, they partook of the world's life to a greater extent. On the next level were the laity. They were of weak moral fiber because they married. (Thanks, presumably, to the weakness of the flesh, the race of humanity was perpetuated.) But even among the laity there were gradations of worldliness. Devout laypersons would regularly go on pilgrimages or retreats to reestablish contact with that which was real. The activity of prayer became those moments in which one turned away from the world and touched the realm of the spirit.

By the thirteenth century, the Hebrew understanding of creation was all but denied. The gothic architecture of the period was designed to sweep us heavenward, out of this world. The plainsong music of this age revealed the incarcerated soul yearning, reaching, searching for the freedom to soar to the realm of the spirit. The art of this time was usually angelic visions or holy scenes.

Life in this world was considered evil unless it was somehow caught up in and blessed by that self-appointed agent of the spiritual realm, the church. Before a Hebrew sat down to eat, he or she blessed God, the creator of the food. It never occurred to the Hebrews to bless the food, for they knew that God had done that in creation. But with the Grecianization of the church, food was part of the realm of the physical, and it consequently was some-how unclean unless proper words or signs were pro-nounced over it. A blessing, to the Hebrew, signified the acknowledgment of God; but a blessing, to the thirteenth-century mind, meant to cleanse, to purify, to make holy that which is profane. Every time well-meaning Christians say, "Bless, O Lord, this food," they reveal that they are still victimized by a point of view quite alien to the bibli-cal story. Food was not the only object that had to be blessed to be made fit for use. Water could not be em-ployed in worship for baptism unless appropriately blessed with signs and words to become "holy water"; this was presuming that water created by God, but not blessed by an agent of the church, was unholy. Bread and wine could not be used in the Eucharist unless blessed and con-secrated to be not just bread and wine, but "body and blood." In these and so many other ways, a huge wedge was driven between the sacred and the profane, between worship and life, between God and the world. Before one moved into a house, it had to be blessed. Before one was buried in the good ground of God's earth, the grave had to be blessed. Before a cross or medal could be worn, it had to be blessed.

A hangover of this tradition lives today in the horse country of Virginia and other places of structured leisure. It is called "blessing the hounds." I shall never forget the first time I was summoned to bless the hounds. In one community where I was serving as the minister, a close friend, who happened to be an orthopedic surgeon, asked if I would be willing to bless the hounds at the Bedford hunt.

I replied, "Jim, there are some procedures in your medical practice that you will not do because they violate your integrity as a physician."

"That's true," he said. "But what's that got to do with blessing the hounds?"

"Well, blessing hounds violates my integrity as a theologian so deeply that I will not do it," I replied. Undaunted by my strange ideas, he called the next most convenient Episcopal minister, who was delighted to accommodate him.

By the thirteenth century, the only way to find holiness in life was to have it touched by or blessed in the name of the spiritual realm. The underlying assumption was that life was not holy, that all its inherent goodness and sacredness had been removed. This was the medieval synthesis at its best. It was a world of order, certainty, faith; it was an age in which time seemed to stand still, and as such it could not finally endure.

From the thirteenth century on, this medieval world was broken down, as it experienced in wave after wave the shocks of modernity. With every shock the realm of the spirit—so overwhelming and dominant—began to shrink, and correspondingly the realm of the physical—so long ignored and disdained—began to grow. There were many factors that combined to make this so: the Crusades, the Renaissance, the rise of humanism, the rise of the physical sciences, the reform movements. All of these and many more produced the modern world. As one might imagine, this modern world had a fantastic effect on the religious mind of the thirteenth century, and medieval thinking was seriously challenged.

Although it is not within the scope of this book to trace these developments in full, I would like to pick three key voices out of this period that can illustrate what was happening to the way people perceived the meaning of their world. They are Copernicus, Charles Darwin, and Sigmund Freud.

Copernicus was a religious man, but one who had an unfortunate habit: he liked to study the movement of the stars. He had scientific curiosity and a mathematical mind. This meant that he allowed the realm of physical reality to engage a major portion of his time, which, according to the thinking of his age, could have been better spent contemplating God or mortifying his flesh. As one might expect, that lack of discipline got him into trouble; for the more he studied the movement of the heavenly bodies, the more he was convinced that the earth was not the center of the universe. Starting with Copernicus, there came a flood of data that effectively removed the world from the midpoint of creation. This earth, he determined, was a minor planet revolving around a middle-sized star in a great galaxy of stars called the Milky Way. Therefore, we human beings were not lying serenely under the intimate stare of the creator-God. In terms of the vastness of the universe, this earth was but a speck of sand.

Such a revelation was a serious challenge to the theological thought of the time, for it diminished the importance of the earth as the center of the universe. It challenged the heretofore unchallenged assumptions of Christian theology. The hierarchy of the church was not pleased, and Copernicus was excommunicated as a heretic. His excommunication notwithstanding, a mortal blow had been struck, and within a hundred years the insights of Copernicus were almost universally accepted. Great new truths began to tumble forth in rapid-fire succession. The institution that believed itself to be the guardian of spiritual reality had been successfully encountered and defeated. The realm of the spirit had begun to shrink; the realm of the physical had begun to expand. In diagram, reality was perceived like this (Fig. 5):

The spokespersons for Christian theology began to retreat, for the first time since the Edict of Milan, into a defensive position. It was as if they said, "Well, perhaps this

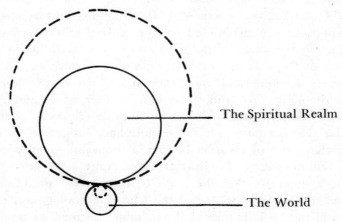

Fig. 5 POST-COPERNICUS WORLD

world is not the center of the universe, but on this earth there is a unique creature called the *human being*, and that creature is the crown of creation, the image of God. Human beings are made just a little lower than the angels, and they enjoy this status because they are the center of God's attention in this whole universe." On this defense line the church rested. Then along came Charles Darwin.

To Darwin, human beings were not just a little lower than the angels, they were just a little higher than the apes. This assertion caused the whole religious establishment to shake violently. It was not only that evolution challenged the newly popular literalization of the scriptures, but it also located humanity deep in the bosom of physical reality. *Homo sapiens* was part and parcel of the world, kin to the lower orders of animals and plants. The human claim to uniqueness was compromised. The science-religion battle was engaged. Its echoes are still being heard today. The Scopes trial in Tennessee was a twentieth-century phenomenon, commanding front-page news in every paper in America. With the administration of Orval Faubus in Arkansas (1955–1967), the teaching of evolution was prohibited in the public schools of that state in the name of defending religious truth. As in the case of Copernicus, finally the insights of Charles Darwin were accepted, and now they undergird every biology textbook in this land. The first chapter of Genesis has been reinterpreted a thousand times in efforts to harmonize that account with the evolutionary insight. Each day in that story of creation became a thousand—maybe even a billion—years. Traditional Christianity was more and more defensive. Yet the truth of Darwin was established, and the old defense line of the Christian apologists had to be abandoned. Humankind no longer seemed so unique, so central, so special, so removed from the world. Once again the realm of the spirit shrank and the realm of the physical continued to expand. The symbolic depiction of reality began to look like this (Fig. 6):

Spokespersons for the church retreated to search for a new line of defense. They found it in what might be called "the spark of divinity." Again it was as if they were saying, "Perhaps this earth is not the center of the universe. Perhaps humanity did evolve through a process of millions of years from lower forms of life; but once human creatures emerged, they possessed souls that made them unique, the inner spark of divinity that united them with the spiritual realm." This was the new line of Christian defense. To fan this spark until it glowed with consuming fire became the purpose of the spiritual life, the goal of the Christian experience. Inner piety became the standard activity of Christian devotion; and here Christianity settled with a tenacious clinging, waiting for the next onslaught with its domain seriously diminished. Then along came Sigmund Freud.

Freud put our human life on his analytical couch and

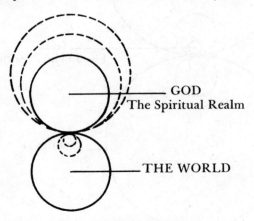

GOD
The Spiritual Realm

THE WORLD

Fig. 6   Post-Darwin World

opened us up publicly, pulling out all our inner secrets, our fears, our phobias, and thus exposing our very souls. Suddenly the inner religious life, the spark of divinity, the soul, was deeply suspect. Religion was challenged as a neurotic extension of parental power designed to keep humanity in a kind of infantile dependency. We were no longer sure we had souls, no longer sure there was a God, no longer sure there was anything beyond the here and now—the world of sight, sound, taste, smell, and touch. Again the realm of the spirit shrank; the realm of the physical expanded, and reality looked like this (Fig. 7):

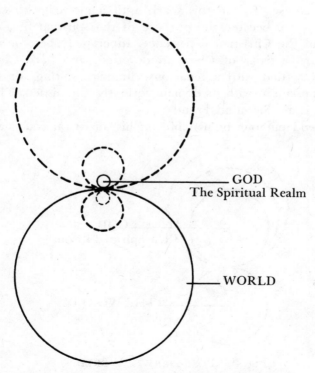

GOD
The Spiritual Realm

WORLD

Fig. 7   Post-Freud World: 20th Century

Since the thirteenth century, God had become what Dietrich Bonhoeffer called a "gap-filler god"; that is, whenever the gaps in human knowledge or experience existed, God was cited to explain the inexplicable. However, the gaps in our age are getting fewer and fewer. With every new scientific discovery, God seems further removed. Thirteenth-century life was centered in the realm of the spirit beyond life, but twentieth-century life is blatantly earth-centered. Ours is a materialistic, scientific age. This world alone is what matters. Today's person is not sure there is any other world. What is important is *now*. The future is too insecure, too uncertain. The good life is no longer found in spiritual perception but in material comfort. "Better things for better living through chemistry." Today's citizens long ago stopped fearing hell; now they have even stopped yearning for heaven. This present life is all they trust.

Today, the realm of the physical is all-important. The realm of the spiritual is almost nonexistent and is reserved for those strange folks who "like that sort of thing." What we have is a very literal reversal of the mentality of the thirteenth century. The "no reform" of the thirteenth century has been replaced by the impatient pressure for reform of our day. "Freedom *now!*" is the cry. Gradualism is a cruel mockery. In the thirteenth century it was the eternal future that was real; life here was unimportant. Today the younger generation calls itself the "now" generation, for now, alone, matters. Today the status of medical doctors is at an all-time high, for they are believed to hold the power of life in their hands. They can prolong this life, here and now, sometimes even to absurd degrees. This life, alone, we trust. Only this life seems real; all else is illusionary.

The realm of the spiritual inherited from the dualism of ancient Greece has been diminished almost to the point of nonexistence. Yet that is the realm in which we have located God, the realm through which we have defined our creeds and our doctrine, the realm from which we created the language of our worship. Now that realm has no power. Finally, someone said: "God is dead!" The god of religion probably is dead (Fig. 8). The Christianity tied to that realm is increasingly irrelevant. The language shaped by that realm is increasingly nonsensical; it no longer translates into our reality. In our experience there is no height, no heaven; no depth, no hell; no escape, no transcendence. Thus, finally, there is no God. Only the realm of the physical world seems to remain: the here and now. Long ago we allowed the dualism of the Greek world to suck all the holiness out of life, all the sacredness, the presence of God, and to isolate these in a realm called spiritual. Then we slowly killed that realm, leaving

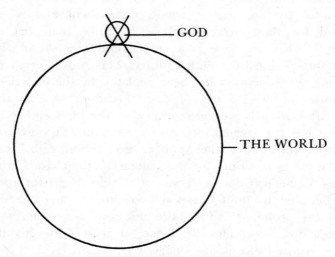

Fig. 8   20TH-CENTURY DEATH OF GOD

ourselves a world that is lost, profane, without meaning or escape. This is where we are today. The dualism is finally gone because the spiritual is dead and only the physical remains.

In this one-dimensional world we search for meaning somewhere beyond the world, and increasingly we do not find it. We react to this predicament in one of three ways.

We may become neohedonists, sinking into a kind of orgy of passion, hoping to find meaning in the search for pleasure. The only goal in such a life becomes the satisfaction of our needs. This is, in part, what lies behind the morality revolution of our generation, the instability of our marriage patterns. Ultimately it is reflected in the sensuous quality of our stage, our cinema, and our novels. There is in our day an intense search for meaning and fulfillment on the level of pleasure alone. The sacred literature of neohedonism adorns every newsstand of this land, depicting the flesh from every angle imaginable. The best known of these publications is *Playboy.* It, along with its imitators, treats human life in a depersonalized way. Human value is determined solely by how much pleasure that person can give. A center foldout of a nude or almost nude woman is proclaimed the "playmate of the month," as if this woman is a thing or a function and not a person. The *Playboy* philosophy is simple: ultimate meaning is found in meeting my needs for physical pleasure. This response to the collapse of transcendent meaning is widely popular in our time.

I remember vividly an experience I had in South America, where I was lecturing to a group of Roman Catholic seminarians in Ecuador. The class had about sixty students, all dressed in black cassocks with black ropes girdling their waists. They were somber, pious, devout

candidates for the priesthood. Lecturing through an interpreter, I turned to him and said, "Would they understand
an example from *Playboy?*" My interpreter asked them:
"¿Ustedes comprenden lo que es *Playboy?*" at which all
sixty faces cracked open in sheepish grins, and the reply
was a unanimous "¡Sí! ¡Sí!" Even the secluded life of a Roman Catholic seminary in Latin America, the garb of cassocks, and the folded hands of pious prayer could not
hold out against the influence of this publication. *Playboy*
symbolizes for me the need to find some substitute for
the meaning we once found in what was called the realm
of the spirit—even if that substitute is only the physical
pleasure principle of satisfying the appetites of the body.

Our second way of dealing with meaninglessness is to
face our despair openly and to seek to be courageous and
heroic about it. I call this a noble neostoicism. I see this
point of view articulated best in the writings of Albert
Camus, particularly in his book *The Plague.* Here the hero
looks at life as it really is, without rose-colored glasses,
and seeks to give it the only meaning he can by pouring
his own integrity out into the vacuum of despair. It is his
way of saying, "I can find no meaning in life, but I will
live as if there is meaning with all the beautiful nobility I
can muster, for the only alternative to that is suicide."

Suicide in some form is the third and, I believe,
the only other alternative. It may not be the overt act of
self-murder. It can be the less permanent but still self-
destructive misuse of alcohol or drugs. I do not believe
the drug culture of our day could have been a possibility
in a believing age, for the use of drugs expresses the
overwhelming need to escape, to "take a trip," to find a
transcendent dimension that we no longer can find any
other way. Alcohol and drugs are the dramatic, but not
exclusive, escape mechanisms of subtle suicide. We can
also, with excessive amounts of food, kill ourselves both

socially and physically. We can kill life through religion. Many a religious fanatic does just that, and makes a virtue out of it in the process.

To make physical pleasure the highest good, to live in stoical nobility in the midst of a meaningless world, to seek some escape partial or complete: these appear to be our choices in a world in which the transcendent seems not to exist.

Many prophets of doom suggest that we are seeing the end of morality and the end of Christianity. They assert that Christianity cannot survive this time of testing. I do not agree. I think we have reached only the end of the dualism, the end of the Grecianization of the church and of the Christian gospel.

I am glad the realm of the "spiritual" is no more. I am glad that the god identified with this realm is dead. We took the holiness out of life. We isolated this god in an other worldly ghetto. Now we have killed that god, and we gather nightly at the divine grave to weep in despair. But a god who could be isolated from the world could certainly not be the God of the Bible or the God of the Hebrews. So perhaps the death of that god is only the death of an idol who masqueraded as God for almost two thousand years. Perhaps this god's death makes it more possible than ever before to peel back the layers of accretion and superstition and to hear anew the Hebrew story of God, revelation, Jesus, Christ, sin, and life. For please note that when we lose the dualism, even by collapsing one of the two realms, once again we have a unity to life. For the first time in at least seventeen hundred years we again perceive reality as whole. The only trouble is that we cannot find the depth dimension that the Hebrews knew was there (Fig. 9). We do not have the sense of the holiness of life, the holiness *in* life, that the He-

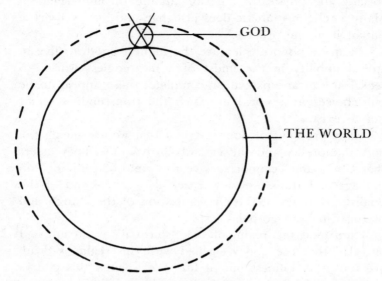

GOD

THE WORLD

FIG. 9 A NONRELIGIOUS WORLD AND THE SEARCH
FOR MEANING

brews had; but we do have the oneness. We live in a
world cut off from its own roots, searching for meaning
but inevitably looking in the wrong place, and so we draw
the wrong conclusion. We search outside life and we find
nothing there.

Many are the voices that want us to resurrect the spiritual realm by artificial respiration. "Back to the Bible!"
they plea. "Back to the old-time religion." But that would
be like doing plastic surgery on a corpse. A much more
radical approach is required. I believe the time has come
once again to introduce this world to the Hebrew concepts of biblical thinking, to lead the religious establishment toward looking at its Lord, its life, its faith with
new eyes—Hebrew eyes. The Hebrews were life-centered,

not life-denying, people. The Hebrews took this here-and-now world seriously just as their twentieth-century, secular counterparts do. The Hebrews appreciated material reality; they suggested that the deeper and more openly one lived, the more likely one was to find that transcendent power we call God. Their passion was life. Their call was not out of life, but into life. This is also a familiar modern cry.

If religion has to do with the realm of the spiritual, then ours is a religionless world, for that spiritual realm is dead. If, in this sense, our generation is forced to choose between being religious and being modern, I hope we will choose to be modern, for any other choice would be neurotic. But I believe that the biblical perspective of the Hebrew mind delivers us from these alternatives. For it was inside that perspective that I was able to see beyond the blinders of the traditional religious frame of reference. There, in a Hebrew context, the ability to love my secular world began to come into focus. Only inside the religionlessness of the biblical story did this Christ figure begin to make sense to me. So we must clear out the rubbish of a religious point of view that is no more, bury the god who is dead, weep no more for that god, and look again at the Hebrew roots of our faith. We look at the heritage that produced the life about which men and women said and still say: "You are the Christ." Then perhaps we will be ready to hear the Jesus story in the thought forms of our world.

However, once I was inside the Hebrew perspective, there was still one serious obstacle that continued to block my hearing. It was the obstacle of moralism.[5] Until that was removed, I did not know quite how a Saviour could save or even make contact with me. In order to remove this distortion that blinds us to the Jesus story, we turn next to look at the preacher's favorite topic: sin.

4

Sin—A Description of Our Being

     I W A S in the ministry of the Christian church for five years before I really understood the meaning of sin biblically. I knew what evil deeds were and I avoided them with righteous passion. I was an incredibly moralistic and consequently an unloving person. Before the Christian story can be heard, the human situation to which the biblical word sin points must be understood. It may be, however, that this word is so corrupted by misuse that it can never be resurrected.

     Yet in the region of my birth, popularly known as the Bible Belt, there is nothing people are more sure of than the meaning of sin. Fervent evangelistic preachers who fill the radio and television airwaves of my beloved Southland rail against it. Sin to them is very clear. It is a bad deed. It is either something you do that you ought not to do (a sin of commission) or something you ought to do but fail to do (a sin of omission). The media evangelists have their favorite anti-sin preaching topics: drinking, smoking, gambling, dancing, going to sexy movies, or "womanizing." The definition of sin involves the knowledge of good and evil and the willful choice of evil. The moralism that such preaching produces is famous for its bigotry and race-baiting prejudice. This is inevitable if life is approached on the levels of deeds that separate the good from the evil. The "good" always feel satisfied with themselves and quite justified in the presumed exclusion of the "evil" from their world.

This deed-level mentality is not limited to the fundamentalist preachers. In a discipline well known in the Christian Church, called moral or ascetical theology, all the bad deeds of life are similarly categorized on a sliding scale. There are mortal sins, venial sins, occasions of sin, and levels of responsibility based on knowledge of sin or extent of involvement. The focus of this tradition is equally on the level of behavior, doing, and deeds. This definition of sin reflects an earlier age of individualism, an age when motivation was not questioned and life was incredibly simple by comparison with our post-Freudian age. The way to deal with sin was quite simply to punish it. The way to deal with goodness was to reward it. Underlying all of life was the certainty that everyone knew and agreed on what constituted sin.

Certainly this was the tradition of my own childhood. I recall being punished for saying such profane words as "gosh" and "darn." I can also remember bedside chats with my mother in which I was asked to swear that I would "never taste a drop of whisky as long as I live." In this tradition, being morally good was equated with being a Christian. A Christian was quite simply one who did not do bad deeds.

When I entered the seminary to prepare for the ministry, this understanding of sin was part of my conscious and subconscious mind. There it was refined, sophisticated, expanded, and altered at least on the surface, but ultimately it was not changed. I saw the gospel from within this limited framework. The Jesus who saved us from our sins saved us from our bad deeds and gave us the power to do good deeds. I began my ministry as a righteous man, a righteous preacher; and there is nothing more difficult for a congregation to bear. I had made virtues out of my vices. I was untouchable. Those who disagreed with me were wrong, unenlightened, perverse—sinners, if you will. Take this attitude and inject it, as I did, into a small town in eastern North Carolina in the late 1950s when the age-old patterns of "separate but equal" racial school systems were just beginning to break down, and you have a recipe for disaster. Yet it was this context that forced me to rethink the biblical definition of sin, to look beyond the level of deeds, to look first at the level of motivation and then at the level of being. Ultimately it was not my doing that was wrong. I was a proper liberal, a champion of the blacks, always on the side of the angels. But somehow my being, my need to vindicate, to justify, to enlighten, to correct, constantly boxed people into defensive shells that made change impossible and hostility inevitable. Life became very lonely until the chasm was bridged by one who reached out to embrace the being that was underneath the deeds. This was the beginning of my understanding of sin as the Bible portrays that great word.

The Bible says: "In sin did my mother conceive me" (Ps. 51:5). Certainly no one can accuse the lusty, life-affirming Hebrews of being mid-Victorian puritans, referring here to the physical sex act through which new life is conceived. No people who include in their holy scriptures a work like the Song of Solomon could possibly refer to sex as dirty or evil.

The Bible says that the sins of the parents are visited

upon the children to the third and fourth generations (Exod. 20:5). Surely something more than deeds is meant here. Paul writes: "God hath made Jesus to be sin for us who knew no sin that we might be made the righteousness of God in him" (II Cor. 5:21). Certainly, in this passage, Paul is using the word sin to describe a state of being, not an act of doing.

Finally, the traditional Christian practice of baptizing infants "for the remission of sin" bears witness to another definition of this word. Very few infants have committed adultery or become drunk or willfully and knowingly violated any of the other popular sins against which the moralists orate.

These glimpses from the biblical story suggest the vast complexity of the word sin. Obviously there are some biblical passages where the word sin means an overt bad deed, but just as obviously there are other passages where it refers to something quite different, indeed so different that it is for me the key first step in understanding with Hebrew eyes the Jesus story.

True to the Hebrew style, our search to understand must begin by looking at life and trying to identify our human experience with nonreligious and nontheological language that might illumine the biblical meaning. What is there about human life that is universally descriptive of our being? What is the inescapable reality of our humanity? What is our uniqueness?

At some point in the evolutionary process, a creature who was called *Homo sapiens* emerged within the natural world. This creature was different from nature and able to stand over against nature. The difference did not lie in an opposite thumb or an upright position, though both of these were of obvious advantage. The ultimate uniqueness lay, rather, in the human ability to transcend the self.

Self-transcendence means that from a vantage point outside the self one can look at the self. Self-transcendence gives human life an awareness of its limitations. This ability separates humanity from the lower animals. Self-transcendence is not an unmixed blessing, for the ability to transcend inevitably produces the reality of judgment. If you can be aware of the self you are, you can also dream of the self you want to be. The dream always judges the reality. The gulf between the two is the source of our human discontent. No creature without self-transcendence can ever know the reality of discontent. Discontent announces the glory and the pain of our humanity. To take discontent away from life, to give us "peace of mind," would be to destroy our humanity. But discontent also feeds our human sense of inadequacy, which, in turn, produces our feelings of insecurity or, in the words of Thomas Harris, our sense of being "not ok." From this reality of self-judgment arises that sense of inferiority we call a "complex" and from which no one ever quite escapes.

As human beings we possess this simultaneous crown and cross of self-transcendence. We develop status symbols in order to minister to our sense of inadequacy. We are compelled to build ourselves up, to announce our worth, to symbolize our importance, to prove publicly our noble ancestry, or in some way to feed our leaking egos.

Our status symbols arise out of the gulf between the self-conscious "is" and the self-conscious "want to be" that marks all life. No person escapes the inevitable struggle to become what that person is not yet. All of us carry a load of self-negativity that expresses itself in our inability to like who we are or to accept what we are.

No one knows this truth of our humanity better than does the advertising industry, for through the media they offer us their products to help us overcome our insecurity. If men feel some anxiety about whether they are masculine enough, they can always minister to that need by smoking a particular cigarette or cigar, or they can be reassured of the strength of their beard. Men complain about shaving, but one has the distinct feeling that the complaint "I cannot go out in the evening without shaving again; it's such a nuisance . . . " is a not-so-subtle broadcast of how masculine he is. So the ads are designed to convince every man his beard is he-man tough—only his skin is allowed to be tender.

Men are not the only targets of the advertising agencies. Women have their insecurity points too in their quest for femininity. The television and magazine ads give them ample help with many products to heighten the feminine form and to remove any potential blemishes. One gets the idea that social success hangs solely on the proper toothpaste, mouthwash, deodorant, or what have you. How can you fail if "you give your mouth sex appeal"?

Alcoholic beverages also have their built-in symbolic value system. Tests reveal that very few people can distinguish between an inexpensive Scotch and the most exquisite brands. Yet having the proper label showing is dreadfully important in advertising one's self-image. It is always a delightful experience to empty the contents of the cheapest Scotch into a bottle bearing the label of the most expensive and place it conspicuously on the coffee table when drinks are offered. The comments are revealing both before and after guests have tasted the beverage. With audible sighs they extol the virtues of that "fine whisky," refusing to dilute it with water or soda. All the time this charade proves only one thing; namely, that people are insecure. Knowing and appreciating good

whisky helps one feel more secure. It was refreshing to
see this theme made overt by the House of Stuart Scotch
distributors, who acknowledged in their ads that their
Scotch was inexpensive and asked, "Are you secure
enough to serve it?"

Even the cereal ads aimed at children on the Saturday
morning television cartoon shows reveal the same human
insecurity. This cereal will make you strong like athletic
heroes; it is "the breakfast of champions." One cereal of-
fers cards depicting big-league baseball players with the
pitch "Be the first in your neighborhood to get a complete set." Certainly that would make any child feel superior. And that is what we all need to feel, because deep
down we all know our inferiority.

We human beings have an interesting way of centering
our feelings of inadequacy on one idea in particular. We
feel inadequate because we are not rich enough, smart
enough, handsome enough, successful enough, fat
enough, thin enough, or whatever else. We pretend that
if we could just overcome that inadequacy we would be
secure. That is a fiction. If we overcame it, we would just
find something else to feel inadequate about. We clutch
these "sweet sicknesses" to our bosoms as the explanation
of all our failures. We hide these secret weaknesses from
all the world. This is why marital conflicts are often so
deeply hurtful. Husbands and wives know the vulnerabil-
ity of their spouses better than anyone else. They know
those hidden weaknesses, those personal sensitive areas, so
in arguments they know precisely where to stick the knife
to make it hurt the most.

In my younger days I felt that all my inadequacies, my
lack of social successes, were the direct result of my pale
complexion. It did not matter that my mother was pale,
my sister was pale, or that my brother was pale. That was

to be rational about my inferiority complex. To me, to be pale was to be less than masculine. I used to look in the mirror and wonder if any girl would ever be willing to go out with a face as pale as mine. This inadequacy was part of my being. Nothing I did seemed to overcome it. A product like "Mantan" had not come on the market when I was a child. I had only feminine cosmetics to which I could resort, but using them was even less masculine than being pale, so they offered no alternative. Even several days at the beach, where I secretly envisioned myself as a sun-bronzed beach bum, left me a color that could best be described as "chapped baby pink." On this paleness I deposited my self-negativity: my inability to love myself, accept myself, be myself. My adulthood is not yet free of this childhood phobia. When I stand at the front door of a church on Sunday morning greeting the congregation, occasionally a sweet elderly lady in genuine solicitude and concern takes my hand, pats it gently, and says, "Mr. Spong, you look sick! You're so pale. Are you working too hard and just can't get out in the sun?" I promise you, it takes all the Christian charity I can muster not to crunch her little hand in mine.

We all have this sense of discontent with who we are, this desire to overcome our insecurity, to prove our worth, affirm our being. Nobody escapes it. Yet it is not all negative, for it also produces in us drive, incentive, accomplishments, monuments to our creativity. There is, however, one other inevitable result. The inner dissatisfaction with life, the insatiable need to *become,* produces without exception self-centeredness. It focuses our attention inward. Inevitably life is organized with ourselves at the center in a vain attempt to meet our own ego needs. We become slaves to these needs, since ministering to them dictates our life-style. We look at life through the prejudiced lens of our self-assigned value. Meeting our ego needs is a primary human motivation. From this universal human discontent comes all of the hurt and pain of life.

We cannot help but operate from a vantage point of what we conceive to be our own vested interest. This is the description of our humanity that underlies one aspect of what the Bible calls sin. Biblical sin is not the account of our doing, it is the description of our being. In Paul Tillich's words, sin is ontological, not moral. There is a vast difference between the two. The Greek word chosen to translate this Hebrew concept is *hamartia,* which means literally "to miss the mark" or not to be what we were created to be. Thus the Bible can say, without being moralistic, "we are born in sin"; that is, we enter existence in the human condition of insecurity. In the human need for power and worth (sin) hath my mother conceived me. This sin, this state of our being, will be passed on to our children to the third and fourth generation. I pass on my insecurities, my fears, my phobias, my inadequate sense of worth, my inferiority complex. All parents observe this in their own children.

If sin is a description of our being rather than our doing, a being we participate in the moment we are born, then suddenly baptism of infants for "the remission of sin" is not as wild or strange a practice as it might have seemed. For every life from birth onward participates in the inadequacy of love, the insecurity of life, the lack of affirmation.

Indeed the analogy of birth is itself a parable not dissimilar to the parable of the Garden of Eden. The fetus from the moment of "quickening," at approximately four and one-half months, is alive in a kind of perfect world. Inside the womb the temperature is constant no matter how wide the temperature variation might be outside. The new life is attached to its mother in such a way that food is always received without the experience of hunger, and waste products are removed without discomfort. There is no loneliness in the womb, for there is no separation. The child is at one with the source of its life. It is a very restricted world in which the child lives, but since there is no other the child has no discontent with these circumstances.

Then, through no fault of its own, the child is expelled from the womb into the world, never again to be apart from need. The world seems vast and hostile. Some stranger inaugurates breathing by holding the child up by the feet and administering a swat. The child experiences temperature variations. The child is covered when cold, uncovered when warm. Hunger is known before feeding, and the discomfort of soiled diapers before changing. Perhaps most significantly, the child knows separation, loneliness, and the need for love that causes one to feel inadequate, unloved, and insecure. The newborn child immediately organizes life to meet personal needs according to the infant's own interests. A set of healthy vocal cords is employed to make the needs of the child known. Mother, father, nurses, grandparents, maiden aunts, and any-one else in the immediate circle become "need-meeters." As needs are met the baby experiences love, which in turn produces a sense of being worthy of love. A loved child becomes a lovable child, for a loved child can begin to love the self he or she is. Only as love and acceptance are experienced can self-love and self-acceptance occur. Only the loved and accepted child can escape in any degree self-centeredness and begin to love and accept someone else. Jesus understood this when he exhorted us to love our neighbors as we love ourselves.

No human life, however, experiences perfect love. No
parent can give perfect love, for no parent can give what
he or she does not have. No human being has all his or
her needs met so that tranquil security is his or her lot.
In the early days of the psychological disciplines, parents
were exhorted to meet their children's needs before the
child was aware of the need. This, they were told, would
result in their children becoming secure adults. Many a
parent tried. But how can a diaper be changed before it
needs to be changed? Life—real life—is an arena where
need is experienced. No one's needs are totally met. No
one is completely loved or accepted. This means that human beings learn in the experience of living that to some
degree they are not loved or not accepted. They translate
this to mean that they are not lovable and not acceptable.
Therefore, they cannot love themselves totally, accept
themselves completely, or be themselves honestly.

Out of this state arises all human self-negativity. Life
feeds it daily. We envision the self we want to be; we look
at the self we are. We seek to overcome our inadequacy.
We cannot escape our self-centeredness. We hide ourselves behind the mask of "let's pretend" because we do
not believe our real self is acceptable. We try to compensate by proving our power and our worth, by building
our status. Self-affirmation becomes our inevitable life-
style, which ultimately binds us into the isolated loneliness
of self-centeredness. This is what sin (hamartia) means
biblically.

What about those overt deeds we consider sins? Are
they not bad, destructive? Yes, of course, they are. But
they are not causes, they are but manifestations. They are
the fever or the rash that accompanies the disease. The
deeds are symptoms of the being. We can take any deed
that we agree is an overt bad deed, drive deep into its

primary motivation, and without fail we discover it to be an attempt at self-affirmation arising out of the insecurity of life.

Consider murder as an example. No one kills unless his or her security level is threatened so seriously by the existence of another person that he or she strikes out to remove the threat—to save his or her being. An overwhelming number of murders in America involve family members or close friends, indicating the truth that people must know someone well to be so threatened that they will hate enough to kill. Even those bizarre psychopathic murders where an assailant will indiscriminately kill a group of totally unknown persons reveal, under examination, that their sick minds saw threat to their being in all those people and they struck out to destroy them before being destroyed by them.

Adultery is no different. Underlying the act of adultery is the insecurity that seeks to prove masculinity or feminine attractiveness or power. Underneath the moonlight and roses of every romance-laden affair is an attempt to boost the ego, to overcome deep insecurities. This is why one refers to the "dangerous forties" in the marriage pattern. The insecurity of growing older, the loss of youthful beauty, the fear of declining virility, the professional affront of watching a younger person advance beyond one's own station in life: these are the forces that create the "dangerous forties" and send husbands and wives searching for ego-fulfillment outside marriage. Adultery is simply another way of seeking to minister to insecurity.

We go on down the list. Lying is an attempt to create a world in which we look better than we are because we cannot accept the reality of what we are. Our lying almost always serves our self-interest. When we lie about the fish we caught, it always grows, it never shrinks. But our golf score shrinks, it never expands. Gossip is our attempt to build ourselves up by cutting someone else down. When we pass gossip along, we prove that we are important insiders to personal revelations. Prejudice is our attempt to prove we are superior. If we really felt superior we would have no need to look down on anyone.

All the misdeeds of creation arise out of our need for affirmation. The exploitation of natural resources or of powerless people reveals our quest for status, wealth, or some other symbol of success and approval. The use of warfare as a means of settling disputes is finally only a tragically childish attempt to get our own way or enhance our "turf."

For the biblical mind, all human evil, all bad deeds arise out of the distortion of human life reflected in our inability to accept ourselves as we are, our inability to live our dreams or our visions. When Paul, in the Epistle to the Romans, tried to explain this, he used three words that are quite distinct in Greek, but are all translated "sin" in English:

1. *paraptōma*—The original sin, the alienation of the creature from the Creator. The substituting of the creature for the Creator.
2. *hamartia*—The state of life in which we live. Life that misses the mark. The life separated from the love that frees one, leaving us shackled in the self-centeredness of our insecurity.
3. *parabasis*—The bad deeds that flow from our fallen state, revealing our sickness.

Using the word *sin* to cover all three concepts is the source of most of the misunderstanding. *Sin* describes our being as well as the deeds that arise out of and reflect on our being.

The Hebrew Bible is the story of the alienated creature—the victim of human insecurity—struggling for affirmation in history. Underlying that story is the Hebrew myth of creation and fall that expressed the Hebrews' deepest insight into and understanding of life.

The world, the Hebrew believed, was created to be perfect—revealing and sharing in the goodness of God. The order of nature was established to be in complete harmony, with everything re-creating itself in perfect balance. The lion and the lamb could lie down together. The man and the woman were at one with each other and with God in the utopia of Eden where there were no needs. Human beings were to be the stewards of creation but there was a limit placed on this humanity. In Eden that limit was expressed by the tree of forbidden fruit. The Garden of Eden was a story of the human attempt to deal with the awareness of this limitation.

Into that perfect garden the snake came slinking through the grass. To the woman the snake said, presumably in perfect Hebrew, "Eve, did God place a limit on your humanity? Did he say you shall not eat from the tree in the midst of the garden?"

"Yes," Eve responded. "God set a limit for us. God said we could eat of every other tree, but if we ate of the forbidden fruit we would surely die."

"You won't die," the snake responded. "God knows that if you eat from this tree you will be as wise as God, discerning good and evil."

Look at the temptation. She would be more than human. To be more than human meant being discontent with being human. She would want to become something else. Eve was intrigued with this idea. The seed was planted. Thus, in this myth, when Eve began to see human life as limited, sin entered the world. Human life no longer seemed adequate to her once discontent was born.

So Eve ate. Because evil desires company, she gave to Adam, and he ate. Then, said the Hebrew myth, "their eyes were opened." Self-transcendence was experienced with its resultant negativity, self-judgment, and guilt. "They knew," said the myth, "that they were naked and they were ashamed." Quickly moving to cover their disgrace with the mask of "let's pretend," they made fig-leaf aprons. They hid that which was unacceptable in their being. They hid from each other. They could not allow their being to be known.

Adam and Eve portrayed all of human life. The God with whom they were once at one, who "walked with them in the cool of the evening," was no longer their friend. They were separated, and in their separation they experienced God as judge. Guilt always creates judgment, for only thus can guilt be alleviated. So when the cool of the evening came and God arrived to walk with these friends, they hid in the bushes.

"Adam, where are you?" God called.

"Hiding here in the bushes," came the embarrassed response from the trapped, guilt-laden creature.

"What in the world are you doing in the bushes?" God inquired.

"I was naked and ashamed, so I hid," came the all-too-human response.

"Who told you that you were naked? Have you eaten of the tree in the midst of the garden?" This voice of judgment was too much for the insecure Adam, and so he did what all insecure people do when they cannot face reality. He rationalized his behavior by blaming his weakness on someone else.

"The woman whom you made gave me the fruit, and I

ate." How wonderfully real and human! We can all identify with that.

A favorite story of mine involves a New Yorker who overslept one morning when he was due to catch an early train. Leaping out of bed, he shaved and dressed, skipped his breakfast, and grabbed only a cup of coffee as he kissed his wife at the door. He tried to hail a cab but the only ones that passed his corner were marked "Off Duty." His impatience rising, he checked his watch and determined that if he walked briskly he could navigate the ten blocks to Penn Station and still make his train. Arriving on foot, he breathed a sigh of relief that his train had not departed. But he also noticed that he was out of cigarettes. He went to a vending machine and inserted the necessary coins. He pulled the lever—and nothing happened. He shook the machine vigorously, but still nothing happened. Reluctantly he reached for more change and again fed the vendor. This time he tried a different brand but with the same result—nothing. As he shook the machine again he heard the last call and noticed his train beginning to pull out of the station. Giving up on the cigarettes, he grabbed his briefcase, which opened, spilling his papers on the floor. Recovering them as quickly as possible, he ran down the ramp to his train, arriving just as it pulled away. He stood there experiencing all the emotional frustration of that moment and then turned to walk back to the waiting room. Inside, a little old lady, whom he had never seen before, was bending over to tie the laces on her tennis shoes. The target was irresistible. He gave her a healthy boot and screamed, "You're always tying your damn shoestrings!" It is so easy, so human, so irrational to blame our shortcomings and our frustrations on someone else.

Adam blamed Eve. Eve blamed the snake. Both had very rational ways to explain and to justify their behavior. Once again the Hebrew myth puts a penetrating finger on our humanity. Our sense of inadequacy, our guilt, produces endless rationalizations. We can explain why we are fat, why we don't stop a certain bad habit, why our affair is different, and so on down the endless list. Rationalizations are our fig leaves designed to cover our guilt, our shame, our inadequacy. They are the direct result of feeling exposed as something less than what we really want to be.

We are created for the perfection of the Garden of Eden. But all of us live "East of Eden." Adam and Eve were banished from the garden and forced to live in the real world of need and sweat, hurt and pain. Human life is to be lived in search of that which can affirm our being, restore us to ourselves, overcome our insecurity. We live in a state of separation from our truest self, our truest being. Biblically, this state of life is called "sin." We are conceived in it, born in it. We pass it on to the third and fourth generation. We yearn to be free and whole. With our being we inevitably cry: "Who shall deliver me from the burden of this sin?"

This was and is the biblical view of life. The Hebrew people articulated this view through their folklore. They sensed that there was in human life a universal yearning to be what all of us intrinsically believe we were created to be. The Hebrews saw human beings as those who refuse to give up their dreams of wholeness, but who also must admit their limitations. Biblical men and women were haunted by their dream of Eden, their image of a lost paradise, a lost perfection. That dream always judged their reality. It always made them dissatisfied with anything else. They knew that no one was able, finally, to be the source of his or her own self-affirmation. No one can create wholeness or bring about a self-restoration to Eden.

We search for life, love, wholeness, freedom, being. We cannot create it for ourselves, though we try. Every overt attempt to win love is basically a self-centered attempt at ego-building and results not in community but in more separation. It was inevitable that the Hebrews who saw life this deeply began to look for the presence of an affirming power that was outside themselves. Ultimately they personalized it, and called it the "Messianic hope."

This power would break the power of sin—"overcome the sin of the world"—by overcoming the broken distortions of human life, by bringing perfect love to the inadequately loved life. It would rid human beings of their self-centeredness by giving them the capacity to accept themselves. It would take away that which stands between every human life and its full realization. It would be a call to be all that we were created to be. For that is the saving work of love.

On every page of the Hebrew scriptures there is this insight into life. Behind all that exists the Hebrews saw the goodness of creation. Superimposed on that they perceived life's distortion, resulting, finally, in a yearning or prayer for restoration: "O come, O come, Emmanuel."

Against this background we want to turn now to the figure of Jesus of Nazareth and seek to understand him in nonreligious language. We want to place him in a Hebrew context. We will attempt to locate him deeply in the Hebrew scriptures. We will examine the Hebrew images whereby men and women tried to grasp his being. Then we will search out the words he used to describe his gifts, and the words others used to explore his power. It will not be a systematic or exhaustive study. But there will be a shaft of light here and another ray there that will illumine him perhaps in a new way. When this task is complete we will seek to summarize his story outside the traditional context. I hope he will be a Hebrew Jesus for this secular generation, a nonreligious Christ, but still the Lord of life.

PART II

❧ ❧ ❧

Some Hebrew Images

5

❖

The New Moses

J E S U S of Nazareth was not born in a vacuum. He came out of a very deep and rich Hebrew heritage. His life was shaped by the military, political, economic, and religious forces of his day. Those forces were the result of a long and noble history of the people in that region of the world. He was of the tribe of Judah. In his body were the genes that linked him biologically to Abraham, Moses, David, Isaiah, Amos, Judas Maccabeus, and countless others. John A. T. Robinson has stated in his book *The Human Face of God* that he was not "a cuckoo who had been inserted into the nest of humanity." He nursed at the breast of his Jewish mother. He learned the carpenter's trade at the side of his Jewish father. He grew up in a Jewish home town, the village of Nazareth. His adult life was spent primarily in Jewish territory, with only occasional visits to the surrounding land of the Samaritans or of the Gentiles.

Jesus was taught the scriptures of his people. He allowed their subtle messages to flow continuously like waves over his conscious and subconscious mind. He studied the law of Moses and used it like a rapier in confrontation with the Pharisees (Matt. 19:7). He knew the Psalms of David and quoted them both in debate (Mark

81

12:37) and in silent meditation, including his dying moments on the cross (Mark 15:34; Ps. 22). He was aware of
both the agony and the ecstasy of his nation. He knew
the grandeur of Solomon's kingdom (Matt. 6:29), as well
as the despair of the period of exile (Matt. 23:35). He
worshiped the God revealed in Jewish history, called by
the Jewish name Yahweh. He himself applied to this God,
for the first time, the Semitic word *Abba* ("Father"), a
word that dramatically expanded the way people thought
of and understood God.[1]

His own ministry was not without contact with or influence from the prophetic movement of the Jewish past.
In his own mind he saw himself in some of the images of
the Hebrew scriptures, and certainly those who had the
task of interpreting his power to the world used ancient
Hebrew images to represent him. I am personally convinced that our world will never see or understand this
Jesus until he is placed deeply into his Hebrew frame of
reference. My purpose in this section is to expose some of
those Hebrew images and allow them to illuminate his
life, his actions, and his words.

The great founder of the Hebrew nation was Moses.
He was raised with privilege in the court of Pharaoh yet,
according to the tradition, he chose to identify himself
with the Hebrew slave people. He suffered their indignities. Their abuse became his abuse. Their slavery became
his slavery. He felt compelled to free this people, to confront the power of Egypt with the zeal of his God. His
purpose was to effect an exodus from bondage and to establish a new kingdom of freedom in a promised land.
The story was told in the biblical account with heightened
miracle and magnificent liturgy.

The sacred Passover meal was the yearly ritualistic
reenactment of the birth of this people as a nation. But

Moses gave them more than freedom; he also gave them shape, form, law, and faith. They made a covenant with this God of Moses at Mount Sinai. They became Yahweh's people. Yahweh became their God. Yahweh was a God of history, not a God of nature. This God was known in life, not outside of life. The divine purpose was the historic task of calling the nations to worship, and in that worship to enable men and women to discover their own humanity. This God was not bound to the cycle of nature—birth, maturation, death, and decay—a cycle that one must ultimately transcend or escape. Yahweh was a God who called human beings into life, who broke the bonds of slavery, who had a word for human disputes, who was involved in the concerns of the people.

Moses made this Hebrew nation a nation of God-intoxicated people, but they were never pious, sentimental, or religious in the traditional sense. The law of Moses, enjoined upon this people by the covenant, spelled out both their duty toward God in worship and their duty toward their neighbor in life. These were inseparable duties—two sides of the same coin. From Moses sprang the heritage and the glory of the Hebrew nation.

It was inevitable that because Jesus of Nazareth came into this tradition he would be seen in the light of Moses, both by himself and by his disciples. This, indeed, was one of the major images underlying the gospel record: Jesus, the new Moses, the greater Moses. This image was most overtly apparent, I believe, in the Gospel of Matthew, but it was subtly obvious in all the other gospel accounts, especially Luke.

Matthew, writing to a Jewish audience, deliberately sought to present Jesus in Jewish images. He was the heir apparent to the throne of David (Matt. 1:1ff). He was the fulfillment of all Jewish prophetic expectation (Matt.

2:23). Matthew was overly enthusiastic in this enterprise, acting very much like a fundamentalist preacher citing proof texts with little or no attention to their context, and sometimes with farfetched results. The life of Jesus that Matthew portrayed repeated the life cycle of the whole Hebrew nation, including a sojourn in Egypt (Matt. 2:15). Lastly, Matthew went to great lengths to present Jesus as the new and greater Moses. The portrait began very early.

According to the tradition of Israel, at the time when Moses was born in Egypt the Egyptian authorities were fearful of the latent but growing power of the enslaved Jews. Responding to this fear, Pharaoh ordered that all Jewish male babies be destroyed at birth. Under this sentence of death, Moses entered life. He was hidden by his mother until he was too big to hide any longer. Then, says the story, his mother placed her infant son in a basket and put him in the bullrushes of the Nile River where the Pharaoh's daughter came to bathe. The result was not only that Moses' life was spared, but also that he was raised in the palace as a son of the Pharaoh by the daughter of Pharaoh.[2] He was given the name Moses, an Egyptian name.

When Matthew began to tell his story to his Jewish audience he chronicled a similar account about Jesus' birth (Matt. 2:16ff). Once again a powerful king posed a threat to the Jewish male babies. Herod, having been deceived by the wise men, sent his soldiers to Bethlehem with orders to slay every Jewish boy under two years of age. (They are known in the Christian tradition as "the Holy Innocents.") Once again the child of promise was spared. The holy family fled to Egypt. No Jewish reader failed to hear Matthew's real point, which was not that such an event literally occurred, but rather that this child was a new Moses whose birth occasioned the retelling of a Moses story.

Matthew's parallel does not stop there. Moses came out of Egypt led by a vision (Exod. 3:1ff), so Jesus was brought out of Egypt led by a dream (Matt. 2:13ff). Moses led the children of Israel through the water of the Red Sea. This was a no-turning-back moment. Beyond that water was a new life, a new vocation, a new calling for Israel. Crossing the Red Sea was the final break with the past, the beginning of something new. Matthew portrayed the Baptism of Jesus similarly, paralleling it quite consciously with the Red Sea moment for Moses and Israel. In the Baptism, Jesus heard a voice from heaven designate him the unique chosen one. He emerged from that water with a new purpose, a new intention. He could never be the same. Much was now clear that had not been clear before. His direction was set. Similarly there was for him no turning back.

After Moses and the children of Israel emerged from the Red Sea, they lived in the wilderness. The book of Exodus tells us the wilderness wanderings took forty years (Ed. 16:35). In this period the nation and its leader wrestled with the implications of what it meant to be the people of God. It was not always an affirming designation. To be the people of God produced fear, pain, and persecution in the history of this nation. It meant sacrifice and deprivation. They were not always certain they wanted to be God's elect.

Once again Matthew paralleled the experience of Jesus. Following the baptism with its specific call to a peculiar vocation, Jesus, like Moses and the people of Israel, went into the wilderness to wrestle with the implications of his new-found destiny, his purpose as the chosen one, the Messiah of God. The wilderness-testing lasted forty years for Moses and Israel. It lasted forty days for Jesus of Nazareth (Matt. 4:2).

When Jesus emerged from the wilderness, he began assembling a band of disciples (Matt. 4:18). Because the children of Israel under Moses had been divided into twelve tribes, Jesus, the new Moses, chose twelve disciples to establish the twelve tribes of the new Israel (Mark 3:14).

Moses next became the lawgiver. The books of the law, the Jewish Torah, were also called "the Books of Moses." The account of the giving of the law was dramatic, fearful, somber. There was a ceremonial act of preparation. The mountain was sanctified. One touched it under pain of death. The giving of the law was accompanied by a theophany—an experience of the presence of God (Ex. 19). Thunder, lightning, thick clouds, smoke, trumpets, all were part of the drama. Then God spoke through Moses from the mountain, and the sacred law was given. The law began with the Ten Commandments, which were followed by ordinances, rituals, directions, and commentary. Specific applications of the universal principles were discussed in detail. The people now had a law that bound them to God and to each other. It was a law that set them apart from the world so that they could achieve their unique purpose to be the people of God.

Certainly, if Jesus was to be the new Moses, he must give a new law. So Matthew, in order to complete his new Moses portrait, gathered a great collection of the teachings of Jesus. He organized it, codified it, systematized it, and paralleled it with the law of Moses. The beatitudes were set as universal principles of the new covenant to parallel the Ten Commandments—universal principles of the old covenant. The law of Moses was divided into five books; the new law of Jesus was divided into five sections.

Moses had delivered the law of God from a mountain, so Matthew took Jesus to a mountain where the new law poured forth from his lips. We call it the Sermon on the Mount (Matt. 5, 6, 7).

I daresay Jesus never delivered this material in this form. It is clearly a Matthean construction. Luke scattered much of Matthew's material throughout his Gospel. Luke's major collection of Jesus' teaching material was given in a discourse on the plain, not the mountain (Luke 6:17ff). Only Matthew, seeking self-consciously to present in Jesus the image of the new Moses, utilized the mountain background. But for both of these evangelists and for their common source, the teaching of Jesus was the new law, from the Messianic figure.

The Mosaic image did not even stop there. It was more subtle in the events of the passion but perhaps even more important. Here Luke, though not writing for a Jewish audience, becomes our best guide, for his passion story best indicates awareness and understanding of the somewhat hidden Mosaic image.

Moses led the children of Israel out of bondage into a promised land. Luke portrayed Jesus as similarly leading an exodus. It was an exodus out of the universal human bondage of "sin" into the new kingdom of God where the fullness of life could be known. Jesus, like Moses, was on a journey, but for Jesus it was a journey from Galilee to Jerusalem, including all that Jerusalem came to mean. This note of exodus grew as Jesus neared Jerusalem. Before Moses reached the promised land of his destination he had to go through doubt, fear, frustration, and even death. It was a long journey. In Luke's story, when Jesus began his journey (Luke 9:51), the promised land was still far away, and he, too, had yet to go through doubt, frustration, and even death. For Moses there was wilderness before triumph. So after the Galilean phase of Jesus' ministry was complete and before the final journey to Jerusalem had begun, Luke portrayed Jesus as going into a similar wilderness (Luke 9). In that wilderness he had another Moses experience, the episode we call "the feeding of the five thousand."

When Moses and the children of Israel were in the wilderness, they were miraculously fed with bread, manna, from heaven. So the Messiah, the new and greater Moses, must similarly feed the host of people in the wilderness with bread, the bread that did not pass away.

One of the important symbols of the Messianic age in Jewish literature was the great banquet, the coronation feast of God. Time and again Jesus used this symbol in his teaching: the parable of the wedding feast, the parable of the great supper. The kingdom was portrayed as a huge banquet with an open invitation. The Last Supper was a dramatic anticipation of the heavenly feast. Luke recorded Jesus as saying at the Last Supper, after he had eaten the bread, "I shall not eat it again until it is fulfilled in the kingdom of God"; and after he had drunk the wine as saying, "I shall not drink again of the fruit of the vine until the kingdom of God comes" (Luke 22: 16–18).

Jesus' exodus, like Moses', would go through a wilderness, only to culminate in a heavenly banquet. The Messianic sign of miraculous manna in the wilderness was retold. The new Moses, whom people were later to call the bread of life, fed the hungry multitude until they were full. So wastefully extravagant was his ability to provide that afterward baskets full of leftover food were gathered.

In Luke's narrative, there were two more episodes before that final journey culminated in the new exodus to the new promised land. There was a discussion with the disciples that began with Jesus' question: "Who do people say that I am?" They answered, "John the Baptist," "Elijah," "One of the prophets of old." "But you," pressed Jesus, "who do you say that I am?" and Peter responded, "the Christ of God." Jesus attempted to fill that confession with its complete meaning. He talked of suffering, rejection, and death. He painted a picture of the cost of discipleship: "those who follow me must be willing to share this suffering, this rejection. They must be so loved, so secure, so free that they can give themselves away. If one hoards this love, it will be lost. If one is motivated to protect life or to save life, that person will cease to live. Both love and life have to be shared or they will die." The revelation of his nature was growing, but the disciples still could not embrace his meaning. They did not understand.

In the second episode (Luke 9:18ff), Jesus took Peter, James, and John up to the top of the mountain to pray. There, the gospel record stated, they had a vision. For the first time their eyes perceived the meaning of Jesus. They saw who he was. It is called "Transfiguration." Interestingly enough, he was seen in the company of Moses and Elijah. With Moses he discussed the "exodus that must take place at Jerusalem" (Luke 9:31), an exodus through death into life. Peter still did not understand. He proposed the erection of three monuments: one for Jesus, one for Moses, one for Elijah. Then the same voice that Jesus alone had heard at the Baptism now was heard by Peter in a cloud that overshadowed him. "Peter, this is my son, my unique revelation. He is greater than Moses or Elijah. Listen, Peter! Understand!" The cloud lifted. Jesus was alone. There had been a dawning of understanding, but nothing was yet clear. Something else had to happen before the full glory of his life could be glimpsed.

Luke knew why they could not comprehend, for Jesus' glory was a glory connected with the new exodus, which was yet to be accomplished.

Jesus' exodus, like that of Moses, was an exodus from bondage, the bondage of sin, the insecurity that binds life, the unlove that destroys life. The accomplishment of this exodus required the free life of perfect love giving itself away. This exodus must pass through the Red Sea of death before reaching the promised land of life. Only through complete love freely given to the point of death could the grasping, enslaving power of human ego needs be broken and life be set free. The disciples could not see this because they were arguing about who among themselves was the greatest. They were still victims of their own self-centeredness, powerless people in emotional chains. So the new and greater Moses began his journey to Jerusalem, his exodus that would lead to the promised land of life, love, and being. When it was accomplished, they would see his glory, and when they saw, they would share in it. His glory was seen in his life—a life so secure that it could be given away, a life so whole and complete it could escape its self-centeredness.

The gospel writers saw in this whole man the source of all life and all love. This life and this love were the power that set him free to be, that defined him for all time. To follow him was to discover this new life, the promised land of being, peace, freedom. His was an exodus beyond even the imagination of Moses. Now with the image of Moses to guide our thoughts, Jesus of Nazareth comes a bit more in focus.

6

❦

The New Elijah

TWO FIGURES from the Hebrew scriptures appeared with Jesus of Nazareth on the Mount of Transfiguration. With both of them he spoke of the departure he must accomplish at Jerusalem. The first was Moses, whom we already have considered. The second was Elijah, whom we shall now bring into our focus.

First let me place Elijah in Hebrew history. Moses led the people of Israel to the brink of the promised land before he died (Deut. 34:4–5). Joshua initiated the conquest that enabled Israel to wrest this land from its inhabitants (Josh. 1, 2). Once the Hebrews settled into the land the only organized structure of government was a confederation of city-states led by local heroes we call the judges. Samuel, the last great judge, was the transition figure through whom this loosely knit people were united into a centralized kingdom. Samuel anointed Saul king (I Sam. 10:1), but he proved to be less than ideal and his dynasty was not established (I Sam. 15:11). So Samuel anointed David (I Sam. 16:13), who together with his son Solomon gave Israel eighty years of prosperity and relative peace. However, the unity of the kingdom never successfully muted the local loyalties, and after Solomon the Hebrew nation broke apart. A rebellion against the central power

of Jerusalem brought about a fracture that was destined
never to be healed (I Kings 12:17ff). The northern half
of this divided land was the setting in which the man Elijah emerged some time during the ninth century before
Christ.

Elijah was a rustic figure in Hebrew history. He was
public and provocative, earning from King Ahab the title
"the troubler of Israel" (I Kings 18:17). He was generally
regarded as the father of the prophetic movement,
though certainly prophets, notably Nathan, antedated him
(II Sam. 12:1ff). Hebrew legends clothed him with immense power: He raised the dead (I Kings 17:17ff); he
closed up the rains in heaven (I Kings 17:1); he tested
God and the prophets of Baal on Mount Carmel (I Kings
18:17ff); he had a magic cloak that performed wondrous
things (II Kings 1:8); he was vengeful and vindictive toward his enemies (I Kings 18:40). In the later Hebrew
tradition it was said that Elijah would precede the coming
of the Messiah (Mal. 4:5; Matt. 11:10); he would prepare
the way. There is no doubt that Elijah imagery colored
the Christian gospel's portrait of John the Baptist. Very
early Christian apologists identified John the Baptist with
the Elijah forerunner (Mark 9:13, Matt. 11:14, 17:10).
Elijah's image shaped the memory of the Baptist's dress,
camel's hair and a leather girdle around his waist (II
Kings 1:8, Matt. 3:4, Mark 1:6). It formed the recollec-
tions of his desert life and even his diet of locusts and
wild honey (I Kings 17:1ff, Mark 1:b, Matt. 3:4). Certainly it helped frame the message Christian writers placed
into the mouth of John: "prepare the way of the Lord"
(Isa. 40:3, Mark 1:3). "There comes one after me who is
mightier than I, the latchet of whose shoes I am not worthy to untie" (Luke 3:16). Obviously there was a deliber-
ate attempt on the part of these Christians to make John

the Baptist fit the Elijah image in order to accomplish their own interpretive purposes.

Beyond this, Elijah loomed beneath the surface of the Christian story as one more image from the past through which to interpret the life and power of Jesus of Nazareth. Here was another startling example of how deeply the Hebrew heritage shaped the Jesus figure and the interpretation of this Jesus figure by the early Christian community.

Interpreting this Jesus was no easy task. The early Christians were faced with explaining a power and a mystery in whose grip they were living. Jesus the Christ had dramatically changed the shape of their lives. His appeal was deep and immense. They looked at him from many angles, but their words could never quite capture their insights. To them Jesus was like the sea beneath the sun. He was always changing, yet he was always the same. They groped for handles to grasp him, concepts to explain him, images to understand him. Inevitably the power of this Jesus eluded their rational thought forms, and so the gospel writers lapsed into poetry, symbols, and mythology to tell their story. Their stories were filled with tales of miraculous power employing the language of symbol. They used poetic, not literal, accounts. They searched for interpretive vehicles designed to capture a truth that mere words could not capture. They did not present the empirical data of scientists, but rather the insights of those who worship, the artistry of believers. We distort the gospel record whenever we fail to comprehend this.

The primary purpose of the gospel design is to lift our vision, not to give documentary photographs to baffle our minds. If we are to understand this Jesus, we must get inside these accounts and underneath these words. In this context it is of the utmost importance to be able to grasp the images of the Hebrew heritage that the gospel writers employed. The image of Jesus as the new Elijah was one of the most provocative, illumining as does nothing else some portions of Luke's narrative.

Luke writing in the book of Acts (1:1ff) gives us the only account of the event called the Ascension. It is not an easy narrative to comprehend. The literal details of the Ascension are nonsensical to modern ears: Jesus rising off the ground and disappearing into the sky like a space rocket in slow motion. This account assumed that we lived in a universe of three tiers in which heaven was the upper tier. No space-age man or woman can possibly believe this. Literally it did not happen! It could not happen! If a literal cosmic ascension is an important part of the Christian story, then the whole Christian enterprise is called into serious question, for such an anti-intellectual religion will not long survive in this technical, scientific age.

But before reducing our options to such bleak alternatives, I suggest a new angle of vision, an angle that reveals this underlying Hebrew image of Elijah, once more deliberately suggesting that only Hebrew eyes will ever be able to embrace and comprehend this Hebrew Jesus.

Again we look at that strange episode called the Transfiguration in which Jesus was seen in a new way. The words deliberately heighten the mystery. Luke said his body was luminous, his clothing radiant like no bleach on earth could produce. Jesus was engaged in conversation with Hebrew heroes of the distant past, Moses and Elijah. But somehow a process was beginning through which the disciples were being forced to see that Jesus was greater than Moses, greater than Elijah. This meaning, however, was not fully appreciated even when the vision was over. Yet from this moment on, Luke was intent on telling his story of Jesus so that his readers would see the truth of this vision. Jesus as the new Elijah began to come into focus. This was the background to Luke's story of the Ascension. If the inner meaning of the Ascension is to be seen we must isolate Luke's presentation of Jesus as the new Elijah. Tracing this thread is a fascinating experience.

Shortly after the Transfiguration episode Jesus and his disciples wandered through Samaria (Luke 9:52ff). They were not well received. James and John, who because of their explosive tempers were nicknamed Boanerges (Mark 3:17), which meant "sons of thunder," were angry. They came to Jesus to inquire if they might call down fire from heaven to consume these unresponsive Samaritans. Those familiar with the Hebrew scriptures immediately recognize the meaning of that request, for on two occasions in the biblical record Elijah had called down fire from heaven.

First Elijah had gathered all the priests of Baal together on Mount Carmel for a contest to decide who the people of Israel should worship (I Kings 18:20ff). Elijah alone represented Yahweh. The test consisted of each side calling to their god for heavenly fire to light the sacrifice.[1] The priests of Baal, four hundred and fifty strong, went first. They prepared the sacrifice and began their ritual incantations, asking for fire to light their altar. They called on Baal all the day long. Elijah, who must have been something of a hair shirt to his enemies, taunted them: "Maybe Baal is asleep. Shout louder and perhaps you can waken him. Or maybe he has gone on a trip and isn't home." Finally, as the sun began to sink, there had still been no answer from Baal, so it became Elijah's turn.

Elijah, displaying a bit of the ham that seems to mark

the professional priesthood, gathered the people near. He laid his altar with twelve stones, one for each of the tribes of Israel. He placed the sacrificial animal in pieces upon the wood. Then he dug a trench around it and proceeded, to the amazement of the people, to pour water over the prospective sacrifice. Three times he repeated the process until it was thoroughly soaked, and the trench around the altar was overflowing. Then Elijah prayed for God to send forth fire from heaven to prove that Elijah's God indeed was God. And, said the narrative, God answered Elijah's prayer. Fire fell from the sky, consuming the sacrifice, the wood, the stones, the dust, and the water in the trench. All the people worshiped in awe while Elijah ordered the prophets of Baal captured and executed.

On another occasion, Elijah, in confrontation with King Ahaziah, called down fire from heaven to consume two groups of fifty people each who were sent to bring him to the king, before he finally relented and accompanied the third group (II Kings 1:9–16). This ability to call down fire from heaven upon enemies of the Lord was a part of the Elijah image that every Hebrew knew.

James and John, still impressed by the Transfiguration, where Jesus was seen in Elijah's company, felt that they were honoring Jesus with their request for heavenly fire to consume the Samaritans. They were suggesting that Jesus possessed Elijah-type power. They, like Peter, who also shared that mountaintop experience, failed to comprehend the meaning of this Jesus.

Luke was using the Elijah image as another way of trying to grasp the greatness of Jesus. But it was only an analogy, never a simile. Jesus, the new Elijah, in contradistinction to the old Elijah, did not come to judge but to save. He did not come to destroy life, but to give life. He was not here to avenge, but to love; not to conquer, but to die. For only thus could he break those powers that enslave human life, powers that only perfect love could overcome. This love revealed the presence of God in human life—not through power, or vengeance, or justice—but through love. This was the recurring gospel theme underneath all the images.

In the Transfiguration episode Luke portrayed Elijah disappearing from the mountain to be replaced by Jesus with his new way—the way of loving his enemies (Matt. 5:44), loving them so much that he would die for them. This was the new concept of God in Jesus, a concept James and John did not grasp at that point. Luke was saying to his audience under these Hebrew images, "One greater than Elijah is here! Watch him! Hear him!"

The Elijah imagery continued in Luke's Gospel. When the time came for Jesus to be "received up" (Luke's phrase), he set his face steadfastly for Jerusalem (Luke 9:51). In Greek the word for "received up," *analypsis,* was the same word used in the Greek version of the Hebrew scriptures (the *Septuagint,* a volume quite familiar to Luke) to describe the death of Elijah when he, too, was "received up" to glory. Recall the account of Elijah's death (II Kings 2:1–12). He was received bodily into heaven, said the Hebrew narrative. He was gathered miraculously in a whirlwind by a fiery chariot, and he disappeared into the sky. "Now," said Luke, "listen to the story of one greater than Elijah. He, too, is going to be received up to glory, and he, too, will disappear into the sky." Luke's readers were invited to watch the process and thus Luke had Jesus set his face toward his destination. He walked his path faithfully, deviating neither to receive the cheers of the crowd nor to respond to the abuse of his enemies. He was going, people thought, to Jerusalem. His procession began with the enthusiasm of Palm Sunday (Luke 19:35ff). It wound past the event of the cleansing of the Temple (Luke 19:45), through the Last Supper (Luke 22:14), the crucifixion (Luke 23:33), and then beyond death to resurrection and new life (Luke 24). He was finally received, not into Jerusalem as even his disciples had expected, but into "glory," into heaven, into the presence of God (Acts 1:1ff, Luke 24:50ff). The portrayal was exact. Jesus was received up into heaven just as Elijah had been (Acts 1:9, II Kings 2:11). Jesus' disciples watched from below just as Elijah's disciple had watched (Acts 1:10, II Kings 2:12).

When Elijah ascended to his glory in the heavens, he bequeathed his spirit to one man, Elisha, his disciple (II Kings 2:15). Elijah's spirit, according to the biblical narrative, represented phenomenal power (II Kings 2:14), and miraculous events were attributed to it. Still, it was the limited spirit of one man. This was all Elijah had to give, and only one disciple could receive it. Luke was arguing through his dramatic portrayal of Jesus' ascension that a new and greater Elijah was here. In contrast to Elijah, when Jesus was taken up he breathed out his infinite spirit on the whole world (Acts 2:1ff). This spirit gathered the scattered apostles, re-created their life, filled them with love and power, and sent them forth to all the world to make disciples of all nations. The Christpower, Luke was saying, was universal, unlimited power. His gift was a gift that filled life full. His spirit brought unity, wholeness, freedom, transforming love. In Jesus, Luke was arguing, men and women could see the fullness of life, and the fullness of life was the glory of God. Jesus, the fully alive person, thus revealed the love and glory of God. The new Elijah was greater, far greater than Elijah.

Hence the Jesus of history and the God who created

history were seen as uniting, for in one the other was revealed. Since first-century citizens thought God dwelt beyond the sky, Jesus had to be envisioned as going to this God, rising to the heavenly tier. This was the meaning portrayed in the story of the Ascension—a story deliberately paralleled by Luke with the biblical story of Elijah. It was not a literal story that we must either accept or reject. It was, rather, Luke's poetic way of saying "the glory of this Jesus is seen when we recognize who he is, participate in his power, and are grasped by his spirit. He is more than Elijah."

To be in Christ is not to be religious, but to come alive. It is to discover the fullness of living. It is to turn on to life. It is to know the power of love. It is to experience freedom from our self-centered bondage. It is to be made whole, to be affirmed. We will reveal the glory of God and share the Christpower of Jesus when we are free to be the self we were created to be, as Jesus was free to be the self he was. Only in this way do we imitate him.

Perhaps now we can begin to see that the story of the Ascension is not an absurd prescientific fantasy. It is, rather, a new way to look at Jesus of Nazareth, to understand him, to respond to him, to find new life in him.

With the help of our Hebrew heritage, with the image of Elijah to guide us, another shaft of light invades the blinders of our twentieth-century vision. The poetic insight of Luke, fed by the Hebrew roots of Jesus' own background, illumines this Christ figure again and again, making it no longer quite so difficult, even in this twentieth century, to call him Lord.

7

❧

The Suffering Servant—
Part I

THE SCRIPTURES for Jesus of Nazareth
were those of the Hebrew community. These scriptures
later became substantially what Christians frequently call
the Old Testament. He studied and quoted these sacred
writings, and he looked in them for the interpretation of
his own life. Apparently Jesus saw himself in some sense
as the culmination of the Hebrew Messianic expectation.
The movement he started was clearly designed to be the
new Israel. He conceived his role to be that of inaugurat-
ing the kingdom of God. Yet his image of Messiah, his
concept of the new Israel, and his vision of the kingdom
of God were quite different from the popular conception
of his day. We cannot help but wonder how he came to
his understanding.

At this point scholars always reach an impasse, for
there are no primary sources. Jesus left no autobiography,
no letters, no papers. There was only the impact of his
life, interpreted by those who spoke of him and wrote of
him. It is impossible to separate completely what Jesus
thought of himself from the categories through which he

was interpreted. Yet having said this, I am personally convinced that no worshiping church or gospel-recorder could have redesigned the whole life-style of Jesus solely to suit their interpretive purposes; and therefore, I feel very comfortable going behind their words to search for Jesus' own understanding.

In this process one image emerges in sharp relief. It is different from the clearly secondary and apologetic images of the new Moses or the new Elijah. This image seems to be deliberately self-imposed, deliberately acted out. It was drawn from the deep and rich Hebrew tradition, but from a part of the tradition that had never achieved domination in Israel. It was the favorite image of some of the smaller splinter groups like the Essenes, as the Dead Sea Scrolls have revealed. This image was the creation of a prophet of the Exile whose writings were attached to the back of the scroll of the prophet Isaiah; hence, this writer is called "Second Isaiah." [1] The image is known as "the Suffering Servant of the Lord." Let me briefly set the historic context for this profound piece of literature.

As we noted earlier, David's kingdom, which brought the people of Israel together effectively for the first time, did not survive beyond the death of his son, Solomon. It became instead two small, jealous, and warring nations. The kingdom to the north, Israel, was made up of ten tribes with its capital at Samaria; and the kingdom to the south, Judah, was made up of two tribes with its capital at Jerusalem.

From the very beginning, the northern kingdom was the least stable. It had no unifying symbol like the Temple of Solomon. It had no established royal family like the House of David. It had no emotional city like the city of Jerusalem. The northern kingdom had no natural defense

lines, no impregnable fortresses. Hence this tiny land was
the victim of military coups, oppressive dictatorships, military disasters; and finally, in 721 B.C., the nation of Israel
disappeared from the face of the earth. Conquered by the
armies of Assyria, most of its people were deported to
Nineveh. In keeping with Assyrian policy other peoples
were imported to Israel for resettlement. These exiled
Hebrews, lacking a principle of unity, simply intermarried
with the people wherever they resettled and soon they
disappeared as an identifiable nationality. The imported
new settlers also intermarried with the remaining Israel-
ites. Their descendants became the "half-breed" Samaritans of the New Testament period, who corrupted, at
least in the minds of the Jerusalem Jews, both the pure
blood of Israel and the pure worship of Yahweh.

The southern kingdom was much more cohesive and,
through judicious political efforts, managed to survive
with some vestige of independence until 597 B.C., when it
was overrun by the Babylonians. Once more there was a
massive relocation of people, with the Jews being forced
to resettle in Babylon. However, among these people
there was a difference: the exiled citizens of Judah and
their children were taught to prepare for and greatly desire the day of return to their sacred soil. They were di-
rected under pain of intense community pressure to keep
themselves apart from the gentile world. Synagogues were
formed to oversee the purity of worship and to instruct
the new generation in the faith and tradition of their ancestors. Sabbath day observance and the rite of circumci-
sion were resurrected from disuse and vigorously enforced
as marks of Judaism. Both customs served to isolate Jews
from non-Jews. Both also served to feed among their cap-
tors the fires of anti-Semitism, which have burned in

varying degrees of shame from that day to this. This Babylonian captivity lasted until 539 B.C., when Babylon fell to the Persian army of King Cyrus and the peoples in exile began to have realistic hopes that they might be able to return home.

It was in this context that the one called Second Isaiah began to make himself heard. He was a figure in exile speaking to his fellow Jews in exile. Part of his message, I believe, was penned while Cyrus was still a hope on the horizon of world history; the remaining part was written after Cyrus was victorious over Babylon and began to allow the Jews to make preparation for a return to their homeland.

About this prophet almost nothing is known. No biographical data were included in his work. He was literally only "a voice crying in the wilderness." But his work revealed a noble mind, a brilliant poet, and unquestionably the Hebrew scriptures' most fluent writer. From his pen flowed a description of a new vocation for the people of God that represented the deepest and holiest level of insight in the entire sacred story of the Hebrew people.

His voice was first raised in the wilderness of captivity: "Comfort ye, comfort ye" (Isa. 40:1), he proclaimed to this broken, despairing people, who were hanging on the brink of extinction, wondering if Yahweh had cast them off forever. Already the Jewish exiles were beginning to seek refuge in idolatry (Isa. 44:17). The thread of racial and religious purity that preserved their identity was about to break. Second Isaiah held before this people the vision of restoration. "Every valley shall be exalted, every mountain and hill shall be made low, the uneven ground shall be smoothed, the rough places shall become a plain, and the glory of the Lord shall be revealed" (Isa. 40:4ff).

When the Jewish nation would be reestablished, he proclaimed, the holy people would find a new hope, a new
idea of their mission to the world.

At this point in the writings of Second Isaiah, exactly
how this would be accomplished and what shape that new
vocation would take were both still vague. Cyrus was just
emerging on the world political scene as a new force. Perhaps in Cyrus, Second Isaiah saw "the feet of him who
brings good tidings" (Isa. 52:7). In this early part of his
work he revealed a pettiness that was not found later. He
still envisioned the restored Judah as exalted above all nations. Restoration would enable this Jewish state to humble her foes and enslave heretofore proud nations (Isa.
41:11, 45:14ff).

But before Second Isaiah finished his writing career,
some historic events occurred. Perhaps in the course of
his writing, Cyrus conquered Babylon, and some of the
exiled Jews, preliminary to a large-scale return, were allowed to go home to Judah. Perhaps this unknown prophet made such a journey; at least that conjecture seems to
make sense out of the data. When he viewed the devasta-
tion and the waste places which were all that remained of
his homeland, the emotional effect on him was beyond
comprehension. The vision nurtured by romantic, nostal-
gic tales and colored by fantasy came crashing down. The
Jerusalem of his dreams, which fed his petty neonational-
ism, and the Jerusalem of stark reality were forced into
confrontation. His holy city was an abandoned pile of
rubble. The Temple was a field of weeds and stones.
There was nothing impressive, no hint of grandeur, no
semblance of power. All his illusions of future greatness
died. Greatness for Second Isaiah could never again re-
side in earthly power.

This experience drove the unknown prophet deep into

himself, his heritage, and his worship. He was forced to rethink the relationship between Yahweh and the chosen people. Most important of all, this prophet had to create another image in order to understand the destiny and mission of this people.

When Second Isaiah finally emerged from this crisis of spirit, the second stage of his prophetic career began. In this stage he sketched his portrait of that servant figure who embodied a higher, grander, more noble destiny for Israel than any Hebrew before him had ever envisioned. Judah was to be the servant people through whom all the nations of the world would be blessed, made whole, and set free. This task would be accomplished not by achieving power but by accepting the afflictions of powerlessness. Second Isaiah intimated that if this role were too difficult for the whole nation of Judah, then perhaps a remnant or even one supreme son of Abraham could fulfill it. As he wrote, this unknown prophet broke the bands of nationalism and revealed what one writer described as "a heart as wide as all mankind." [2] It is obvious that in this portrait Jesus of Nazareth saw himself, and by this pattern he deliberately styled his life.

As this striking servant figure emerged in the writings of Second Isaiah, his task was seen to be that of going beyond the covenant people as an agent for bringing justice to the Gentiles. He would be used by Yahweh to give light and salvation to the world (Isa. 49:6). His mission was universal, not nationalistic (Isa. 49:6). His task was to express the tenderness of God for all humanity (Isa. 42:6), to liberate the suffering (Isa. 61:1), to guide the thirsty to water (Isa. 44:22ff), to set human life free (Isa. 42:7), to make them whole (Isa. 55:1ff, 42:7), to break the power of sin (Isa. 53:12). He would impart God's law to the world (Isa. 51:4); yet this law would not be forced on the

human family, it would rather be presented so that all
would eagerly seek it (Isa. 42:4).

The Suffering Servant would accomplish this task by
working meekly (Isa. 42:1ff). He would be self-effacing.
Though he might be clothed with heavenly power, he
would use it gently. He would not resist hostility or draw
back from maltreatment (Isa. 50:5, 6). This was not
meant to imply weakness, but rather gentle humility. His
face would be set like a flint toward his purpose (Isa.
50:7). He would walk in the confidence of Yahweh. He
would be afflicted, but he would trust his final vindication
(Isa. 52; 53). At the last, the Servant of the Lord would
be overwhelmed (Isa. 53:8). He would meet a shameful
death. In derision he would be slain as a criminal (Isa.
53:9). Nevertheless, God would reverse the sentence of
death, and he would go on uninterrupted until he accomplished his task of bringing all people into unity with
God, with each other, and with themselves (Isa. 53:10ff).

It is difficult to read these words today without being
astounded that in 540 B.C.E. a Jewish writer could produce this profound vision of life's meaning. Nothing like
it had appeared in the Hebrew scriptures before. Having
sketched this figure, the author interpreted the effects of
the Servant's life. Poet that he was, he did not just say it;
rather, he put the interpretation of the Servant into the
mouths of those who witnessed his fate (Isa. 52:13–53:12).
They were not obscure people, for the seeming tragedy
of the Servant's life was enacted on the vast stage of the
whole world. So he was seen as the bearer of our sicknesses, the carrier of our sorrows, wounded for our transgressions, bruised for our iniquities. "With his stripes we
are healed" (Isa. 53:5). His was a vicarious suffering. As
people derided him, the Servant made intercession for
them. By his "sin" offering, his willingness to accept

abuse, he drained the world of anger and thus men and women were brought to peace and wholeness (Isa. 53:12). All of this was willed by God as the way of restoring creation to its glory, said the unknown prophet called Second Isaiah (Isa. 53:12).

God's love went out to this Servant figure, for he stood with God over against evil. The Servant's spoil was not the honor and prestige that motivates the insecure of life. He was free of that bondage. His spoil was men and women won to God—forgiven, healed, justified (Isa. 53:12). When people understood the meaning of his suffering, the Servant would rise up to bless them with his spirit, his life, his presence.

Nowhere else in the sacred story of the Hebrew people was the portrait drawn of the vicarious sacrifice of the innocent out of love for the guilty. Nowhere else was the promise given that vicarious love would bring healing. Yet such was the vocation that Second Isaiah believed devolved upon the people of God when they returned from the Exile to their homeland. It was to be their task to serve the world in self-effacing ways, bearing the world's pain, renouncing all claim to worldly power, and in this way leading all people to light, life, and wholeness. It was their vocation to be a light to lighten the Gentiles. This was to be the glory of Israel.

When Second Isaiah finished his writing, his words fell into disuse and disregard. His vision of the purpose of the chosen people was not the popular one. The Jewish state was much more moved by the religious nationalism of Nehemiah or the exclusive religious bigotry of Ezra as these writers resurrected the dream of earthly grandeur—kings on great horses overturning their enemies.

In the first century, however, a Jewish rabbi named Jesus of Nazareth found these words interpreting his own life and work, but by that time this image was so lost that no one else could see the Messiah in this stance. Yet in the mind of Jesus, the role of the Suffering Servant was always one option to enable him to accomplish what he believed his Messianic vocation to be. He finally chose it, overtly and deliberately, when all other avenues were closed to him and when his purpose seemed all but defeated. This was the biblical image cut from the tradition of the Hebrew people that most deeply undergirded everything Jesus said and did. If this image can be isolated, then Jesus as the Christ will be understood in a new light.

Now we turn to bring the story of Jesus into focus through this image.

8

❦

The Suffering Servant—
Part II

I N   T H E Gospel of Luke alone there are twenty-nine points of reference that seem to indicate the influence of Second Isaiah on the life of Jesus. They range from hints given by similar wording to direct quotations. There is no escaping the conclusion that the Servant passages of Second Isaiah became a primary image through which Jesus of Nazareth came to be understood. The only question is whether this was an image placed upon him later by the Christian community, or whether Jesus himself consciously and deliberately incorporated this image and dramatically lived out the Servant role as the only way to accomplish his purpose.

In the previous chapter, I suggested that to me the last possibility is the more realistic. Since Luke's Gospel most clearly portrays Jesus as the Suffering Servant, I shall examine that image primarily through the eyes of this evangelist.

Luke had hardly begun his story when the first echo of Second Isaiah was heard. It came in the birth narrative when the infant Jesus was presented to the old priest,

Simeon, in the temple. Simeon sang a song called "Nunc Dimittis." Most scholars agree that this song was a liturgical creation by the church that had been placed on Simeon's lips. The content significantly reflected the thought of Second Isaiah, and the line "a light to lighten the Gentiles and the glory of thy people Israel" (Luke 2:32) was almost a direct quotation from the Servant passages (Isa. 49:6; 60:19). Simeon then turned to Mary and spoke to her specifically about the role of this child. "This child is set for the fall and rising of many in Israel and for a sign that is spoken against and a sword will pierce through your own soul also" (Luke 2:34–35). This was the opening prelude to Luke's story of the Messiah who would walk the path of suffering and be shadowed by a cross. The portrait of the Servant figure was coming into focus.

In the other childhood stories that only Luke told, the evangelist went to great lengths to inform his reading audience that Jesus was a child of the scriptures. His parents, Mary and Joseph, meticulously followed the requirements of the Jewish law. The child was circumcised on the eighth day (Luke 2:21). The rite of purification and presentation in the Temple was observed "when the time came" (Luke 2:22). Only when "they had performed everything according to the law of the Lord" (Luke 2:39), did they return to their home at Nazareth in Galilee.

Luke observed that this family celebrated the Passover every year (Luke 2:41), and that when the time came the twelve-year-old boy Jesus was taken with them to Jerusalem in preparation for his Bar Mitzvah. Jesus was pictured as sitting among the learned scribes and doctors of the law engaging in questions and answers, indicating a depth and a profundity not normally anticipated in one so young. The boy was totally immersed in the Hebrew scriptures. The heritage of Israel was his heritage. This was symbolized dramatically as the child Jesus, even on this first trip to Jerusalem, staked a claim to the Temple. It became "my Father's house" (Luke 2:49). Some years later he would do so again. Then Jesus returned home and was obedient to his parents, while he "increased in wisdom and stature and in favor with God and man" (Luke 2:52).

This Jesus is met next when he exploded onto the stage of the world in the story of the Baptism. Luke dated the moment carefully: it was in "the fifteenth year of the reign of Tiberius Caesar when Pontius Pilate was governor of Judea" (Luke 3:1, 2). Now, out of obscurity, stepped the forerunner proclaimed by Second Isaiah. His name was John the Baptist. The words he uttered were direct quotations from Second Isaiah. He was a voice in the wilderness crying, "Prepare ye the way of the Lord" (Luke 3:4ff; Isa. 40:3). Luke clearly saw John the Baptist as the one who opened the door for the Suffering Servant figure to emerge. The self-effacing words of John make this crystal clear: "He who is mightier than I is coming, the thong of whose sandal I am not worthy to untie. He will baptize with the spirit and with fire" (Luke 3:16). The clear contrast is that John baptizes only with water.

To this voice in the wilderness Jesus came. He was baptized (Luke 3:21), thus placing himself inside the movement of national repentance that actively fanned the Messianic hopes. As the baptism experience was related by Luke, it could not be understood apart from Second Isaiah.

There was a vision, an insight. The heavens opened. The curtain that divided humanity from God was parted. In rabbinic literature, the sound of a voice from heaven was likened to the cooing of a dove. In this episode that

dove was literalized, and it descended upon Jesus as the
voice said, "Thou art my beloved Son; with thee I am
well pleased" (Luke 3:22).

These words were a composite quotation from two sacred Hebrew sources, Psalm 2 and Isaiah 42. Psalm 2 was
a hymn of praise proclaiming the accession of a king. Isaiah 42 was the first moment in the prophet's story that
the Servant figure stepped out publicly. "Behold my servant whom I uphold, my chosen in whom my soul de-
lights. I have put my spirit upon him" (Isa. 42:1).

Luke thus clearly identified Jesus with the Servant figure of Second Isaiah. That figure, said Second Isaiah,
cannot accomplish his purpose without suffering indignities, rejection, and finally death.

Luke suggested that all of this broke in on the conscious mind of Jesus of Nazareth at the Baptism, and he
accepted it. From this moment on he saw himself as
uniquely related to God. He believed himself to be chosen
by this God, affirmed and called to the Messianic vocation. His task was to bring others into this relationship,
the marks of which were life, love, freedom, peace. He
saw the world in bondage to sin, a bondage that only
God's love could break. He also began to see that perhaps
the only way to accomplish his task was to live out the
Servant role sketched by Second Isaiah; but that was not
yet a certainty. Time and again Jesus appeared to consider alternatives through which life and love could be offered to the world. Time and again he was thwarted and
forced to return to the Servant image.

Underlying what we call the temptation story was Jesus' searching to understand the meaning of all that happened to him at baptism. The temptation produced no
positive answer. The various options of fulfilling his purpose were simply rejected, and the search went on. The

Messianic task was to bring love, affirmation, acceptance, forgiveness, life to every child of God. To do this was to do nothing less than to bring God to men and women. If this were accomplished, people would inevitably see God in the Messianic figure who brought this love. These were the thoughts that, I believe, occupied the mind of Jesus of Nazareth. He knew what his call was, though he was not yet certain how to accomplish it. The model of the Servant from Second Isaiah was, however, never far from his consciousness.

When Jesus came out of the wilderness where the temptation was faced, he made his first public appearance in the synagogue of his home village of Nazareth. He stood up to read the scripture. They delivered to him the scroll of the prophet Isaiah. He unrolled it to the sixty-first chapter. From the Servant passages he read of the Messianic purpose:

> The Spirit of the Lord is upon me,
> Because he has anointed me to
>   preach good news to the poor.
> He has sent me to proclaim release to
>   the captives and recovering of
>   sight to the blind.
> To set at liberty those who were
>   oppressed.
> To proclaim the acceptable year of
>   the Lord.
>   (Isa. 61:1ff; Luke 4:18, 19)

He rolled up the scroll and sat down. Luke wrote that all eyes were glued to him. He responded, "Today this scripture has been fulfilled in your hearing" (Luke 4:21). This was clearly Jesus' self-identification with the Ser-

vant image. "I am the servant of the Lord," he was saying. "The love of God in me can affirm those who think
little of themselves, those who believe they are the poor
and have no value. My love can set human beings free—
free to be." That was his claim, and that was what he began more and more to act out in his life. His hearers
were dumbfounded. "This man the Suffering Servant?
The Messianic figure? Why we know where he comes
from! He is the son of Joseph the carpenter" (Luke 4:22).
Their eyes could not perceive the true origin of his power. Their ears could not hear beyond his seemingly blas-
phemous words. Hence rejection was the result of this
first public identification of Jesus with the Servant figure
of Second Isaiah (Luke 4:29). From this point on, it was
much more subtly acted out.

When the paralytic was let down through the roof to
the feet of the rabbi from Galilee, Jesus startled the as-
sembled host by saying, "Young man, your sins are forgiven you." The crowd roared, "Who can forgive sins but
God alone?" (Luke 5:20ff). Who but the Servant of the
Lord in Second Isaiah, who became the agent through
which "transgressions are blotted out and sins no longer
remembered" (Isa. 43:25).

When Jesus gave the Sermon on the Plain (Luke
6:20–26), Luke's version of Matthew's Sermon on the
Mount, his beatitudes and woes seemed to reflect the
words of Second Isaiah, who promised food, drink, and
joy to the righteous and deprivation to the unrighteous
(Isa. 65:13).[1]

When the Galilean phase of Jesus' ministry drew to an
end, he prepared to march toward Jerusalem. There was
a note of deliberateness about it. In some sense his hand
had been forced. The hostility had mounted. Herod was
seeking him. John the Baptist had been executed. Jesus'

movements were somewhat curtailed. There was some apprehension that he might be arrested and even die outside Jerusalem. That notion in no way fitted into Jesus' plan. He must confront his nation with his demands and his claims at the nation's heart, Jerusalem. Therefore, said Luke, he "set his face" (Luke 9:51) to go to Jerusalem. It was an interesting choice of words. In Second Isaiah the Servant figure also resolutely moved to his vocation with confidence that, come what may, the final vindication would be his. Not coincidentally Second Isaiah said of the Servant figure, "Therefore I have set my face like a flint" (Isa. 50:7). The Servant went to kindle a fire (Isa. 50:11). John the Baptist said at the beginning of Jesus' ministry, "I baptize with water. He shall baptize with the Holy Spirit and with fire" (Luke 3:16).

Other parallels between Jesus' teaching and the role of the Servant abound. In the parable of the house divided, Jesus talked about what happened when a "stronger person" assailed another, overwhelming "the armor in which he trusted—and divided his spoil" (Luke 11:22). In the writings of Second Isaiah, the strong figure was the Servant who took on evil and, even though he was destroyed by that evil, ultimately became the means whereby bonds were loosed and men and women were presented to God free and whole (Isa. 53:12).

When Jesus, on his fateful last journey, arrived at the edge of Jerusalem prior to the Palm Sunday procession, he gathered the twelve together and said, "Behold, we are going up to Jerusalem, and everything that is written of the Son of Man by the prophets will be accomplished" (Luke 18:31). There was no doubt that the Isaiah portrait of the Servant of the Lord was the primary writing of the prophets that Jesus had in mind. The Servant figure in Isaiah was the one who took on the pain, the hostility, and the bondage of the world. He met each moment with love. He even allowed himself to be killed that others might see how deep the power of love really was. Certainly Jesus' trip to Jerusalem was exactly that kind of dramatic living out of the Suffering Servant's role.

When Jesus entered Jerusalem, his first act was to cleanse the Temple, reclaiming it for his God. He did so with the words, "My house shall be a house of prayer" (Luke 19:46), a quotation from Second Isaiah (Isa. 56:7).

At the Last Supper, after the meal was completed, Jesus watched as the disciples debated which of them was the greatest (Luke 22:24). He said that Peter would deny him. He reminded the disciples that when he sent them out on mission with no provisions they still lacked nothing. But now he enjoined them to a vigorous preparation. "For," he said, "this scripture must be fulfilled in me, and he was numbered with the transgressors, for what is written about me has its fulfillment (Luke 22:37)." Those words, of course, were from the heart of the Servant passages of Second Isaiah (Isa. 53:12). Jesus died, Luke recorded, as a criminal, executed between two thieves (Luke 23:32).

Finally, in Luke's resurrection narrative, it was a recounting of the scriptures that opened the disciples' eyes on the road to Emmaus (Luke 24:13ff). Those scriptures could be nothing other than Second Isaiah, for nowhere else in the Hebrew Bible was the portrait drawn of a Messiah who, through suffering and death, set people free and received God's vindication. The risen Christ commissioned the disciples to go to all people with this message of love and freedom (Luke 24:47). One task of the Servant in Second Isaiah was to break the bands of nationalism so that all might dwell in unity with God, with each other, and with themselves.

When people are loved they will share that love until all others are included. When people are forgiven they will share that forgiveness. When people are accepted they will share that acceptance. When love fills life full, the truest self, the deepest life is free to be and to live. That life has heard the gospel, not just with its ears but with its being. It is a gospel dramatically shaped by the most beautiful and profound image in the Hebrew heritage—the Servant of the Lord found in the writings of Second Isaiah.

Now our story moves beyond the images of the Hebrew tradition to examine key words attributed to Jesus in which he defines himself or through which others came to explain his life and his power. These words are windows to the heart of the Christian story, meriting our serious attention.

PART III

❦ ❦ ❦

Some
Interpretive
Words

9

✤

I Give Rest—
I Give Peace

H E W A S at rest. He lived in peace. He promised rest and peace to his disciples.

It has been our intention to break the fetters of the past that have bound Jesus of Nazareth and to set him anew in the Hebrew heritage from whence he came. Now we must attempt to translate him for our time. Our approach will not be the traditional one, for the traditional approach is part of the problem of our day. Theological words are untranslatable to so many citizens of the secular city called the twentieth century. The language of our liturgy and of our hymns is filled with phrases that we dare not think about too seriously lest we either twist our minds into unrecognizable shapes or abandon altogether the whole Christian enterprise. Traditional religion has forced us to develop an uncanny capacity to shut off our thinking processes in worship, thus making Jesus increasingly unreal.

In searching the Bible with Hebrew eyes, another approach seems to suggest itself through which we might focus anew on this unique figure in whom people saw the power of Christ. We will examine key words that Jesus used, explore their background, interpret what he meant by them and what people experienced when these words were heard.

As we have already noted, however, words are not historically clean. They change their meaning radically over the ages. If words are to help us see the Christ figure, they must be scraped clean, placed in their historic setting, and translated anew for our time. Then they will assist our discovery of the Hebrew Christ for our generation. In this chapter we examine the words *rest* and *peace*.

"Come to me all who labor and are heavy laden, and I will give you *rest*. Take my yoke upon you and learn from me. For I am gentle and lowly in heart, and you will find *rest* for your souls" (Matt. 11:28–29). This is Matthew's Jesus who is speaking. "*Peace* I leave with you; my *peace* I give to you; not as the world gives do I give to you" (John 14:27). This is John's Jesus who is speaking.

Matthew and John bore witness to the fact that in the Christian community of the first century rest and peace were seen as the promised gifts of Jesus of Nazareth; and because these gifts were found in him, they called him Lord. If we can discover the inner meaning of these words and then see them as the gifts of Jesus of Nazareth, we will have succeeded in opening new doors through which we might approach this life. Perhaps then we too can stake for him a claim—a modern claim to the titles Saviour, Lord, Christ.

Biblical rest had nothing to do with comfort and ease. "The Church of the Heavenly Rest" was hardly a title a biblical man or woman would have used. Biblical peace was not sentimental tranquility, or the absence of conflict. It was not the peace that passeth tranquilizers, but the peace that passeth understanding. It was not found in the self-hypnotic trance of the peace-of-mind cultists. What these words rest and peace pointed to biblically was nothing less than the most coveted qualities of every human being.

We begin our definition of these words by searching the Hebrew context and this inevitably forces us to look again at human life. The species *Homo sapiens* consists of creatures with limits. They are unwilling to accept the fact that they are only animals. They are insulted if called beasts, even handsome beasts. They are offended whenever basic humanity is violated by inhumane treatment. They use the names of animals as insults. When a fellow human being is called a dog, a snake, a rat, a chicken, aspersions are being cast on that person's character. We *Homo sapiens* live under a self-imposed standard and expectation that is not applied to any other animal. We are made to be responsible for our behavior. Our actions indicate that we believe that humanity possesses the freedom to control its own destiny. If a man or a woman sinks beneath the level of behavior acceptable to the definition of a human being, he or she is treated as one who is insane.

Humanity is bounded on one side by the animal world from whence it has emerged but by which it cannot be defined. Facing this boundary beneath humanity all people are then forced to recognize and to admit that they have freedom, responsibility, and self-transcendence.

When human beings look away from the animal world toward the other edge of humanity, a different boundary becomes clear and distinct. Human beings are not gods. We are finite and limited, not infinite and limitless. Human kingdoms do not endure, they rise and fall in the tides of history. Like all creatures, human beings die. Our life is not eternal. This boundary between the human and

the divine is as real as the one that separates humanity
from bestiality. If representatives of the species *Homo sapiens* ever forget this limit and pretend to be more than human—superhuman or divine—they immediately become
less than human—demonic, sick. History's bloodiest chapters are written by human beings who forgot this boundary and pretended to play God with the lives of people
and with the fate of the world. Thus any attempt to de-
fine humanity must recognize finitude. Humanity must be
seen as limited by the reality of death, which forever separates human life from the realm of the eternal, from
sharing the life of God.

Human beings are creatures who are unwilling to be
animals and yet not able to be gods. Once these boundaries are recognized, then we can begin our definition of
human life and the other characteristics of the human being can be identified.

The next obvious fact to observe is that no human life
seems content. To be human is to envision a self bigger
than the self we are, a world larger than the world we experience. The gulf between our being and our dreams appears to be eternal. In this gulf human life is lived amid
the peculiarly human frustrations of unrealized hopes and
unacceptable reality. It is here on this level that the biblical words *rest* and *peace* begin to translate, but the human
context must be laid bare even further.

From the moment of birth to the moment of death
life is potentially an ever-widening experience. In both
physical circumstances and mental comprehension, our
world and the self we are can expand. To be who we are
and to become who we shall be are always our realities.

We move from the highly bound security of our mother's womb, where first we experience life, into the vastness of time and space that adults must embrace. This is a

tremendous stretching of our being. Life is a series of expanding frontiers that we are forever called to cross. Every crossing is something of a death and resurrection. Every crossing says at least a partial "no" to what we have been and a new "yes" to what we shall be. It means new vision, new insights, new humanity. But it also means new anxiety, new fear, new insecurity.

We grow from childhood to adolescence to maturity to the middle years, through the aging process, and on to the threshold of death. We go from life in a small social unit called a family to the community school to a college, usually away from home, and on to the ofttimes nomadic and ever-changing adult world that embraces every language and culture and racial group. We move from the perspective of a child clothed only with the family's point of view to one that reflects the regional prejudices of the area, to one that shares the national prejudices of one's country, and finally to one that embraces world concerns. These are only a few of the frontiers that we must cross in our pilgrimage to get from what we are to what we are meant to be.

On each level of our life, after crossing each new frontier, we build for ourselves a security system. We live in that system until, like the darkness of the womb or the shell of a cocoon, it binds our potential and is no longer able to contain our life. Then we must choose whether to accept those limits and die to what we can become, or to leave that secure place behind and cross another frontier. Life grows and expands only so long as we are able to cross from one level to the next.

Finally, there comes, for many of us, a new frontier that we are unwilling to cross. A new insight, a new truth, a new vision of reality challenges our previous view of life, and we discover that to cross that frontier is too painful. Our being is not secure enough to give up our previous support network. So we say "no" and, closing the door, we refuse to walk into that new arena. At that moment our human potential begins to decline. Our world has touched the edges of its final limits. We settle down to live within these hardening, if not yet permanent, boundaries on our being.

Once we have said "no" to a vision, we are never the same. For when we see a frontier that we have refused to cross or a truth that we have declined to embrace, the security of our life is threatened. What we have decided to be is judged by that which we refused to entertain or take into our lives. Hence we seek to repress that uncrossed frontier from our memory. This creates that all-too-human quality of defensiveness about our values. We have to guard them from any possible doubt or erosion. This is what creates fanatics who are unable to deal with the new or the challenging except by ridicule or hostility. Finally this leads to witch hunts or tests of orthodoxy. I heard a clergyman say once that there was only one bishop in the entire Episcopal Church whose theological orthodoxy he trusted. That statement said almost nothing about the Episcopal bishops. But it said volumes about that clergyman. Behind the Bible-quoting religious fundamentalists who are as certain of their truth as they are hostile to anyone who might deviate from that truth there are closed lives of uncrossed frontiers. Behind the anger of the unwavering and unreconstructed racists, behind the defensive tradition-bound spokespersons for the virtues and habits of yesterday, there are these barriers of repression, this refusal to step into a new world that beckons, this inability to leave one security system for a new being.

It is not surprising to me that religious certainty, racial

bigotry, chauvinism, and superpatriotism are often found in the same personality, for all are symptoms of the same disease. When we are unwilling to become, we inevitably exhibit defensiveness about our being. Out of this experience of our humanity, we look anew at the biblical words *rest* and *peace*.

"Come unto me and I will give you rest." Rest is the capacity to accept ourselves in every stage of life. It is the kind of acceptance that enables us to affirm what is. Biblical rest is the child's joy and contentment to be a child in all of the exuberance and vitality of childishness. It is the adult's willingness to love and accept the full responsibilities of adulthood. It is the beautiful dignity of one who accepts the aging process with grace, seeking neither to hasten the end of life nor to slow it down artificially. The rest promised by Jesus of Nazareth is the rest of self-acceptance, the capacity to face the reality of our human situation. It is the ability in any stage of life, at any moment, to love and enjoy the self we are without apology and without boasting. We have rest when we know affirmation so deeply that we are free to accept our own being. In Jesus' words "Come to me for I give rest" there is the claim that he has the capacity to bring us this kind of rest.

"My peace I give to you, but not as the world gives." Biblical peace is that inner security, that self-knowledge, that enables us to cross any new frontier. It is the capacity to live in any world, to respond to any dream. Biblical peace is not like the world's peace. It is not the absence of tension or conflict. The world's peace is found in building bigger and better security systems around us. It consists of status, recognition, and power that ultimately makes us slaves of the system and exhausts our energies in a never-ending struggle to defend our "peace." There is not enough honor or recognition in the world to satisfy completely any human life. Beyond every achievement there are new fields to conquer, new comparisons to make.

Biblical peace is an inner security of being that enables us to accept the discontent of our humanity, to live in the tensions of life without being victimized. Biblical peace is seen in our capacity to rise and fall on the ladder of importance without being puffed up with our successes or destroyed by our failures. It is seen in our ability to leave any security system, to walk unafraid into any tomorrow, to embrace any new insight, and to live in any brave new world.

Full human maturity is achieved in the combination of rest and peace. Rest is the capacity to be. If the capacity to accept the ultimate limits on our humanity, rejoicing in what we are at every moment in every stage of life. Peace is the ability, within those ultimate limits, to become. It is to have the ability to cross frontiers and to experience new being.

This is what it means to have rest and peace as the Christian gospel defines these words. How very different from what the traditional language of religion would have us believe these words mean.

Rest and peace are the promised gifts of Jesus of Nazareth. His claim, or the claim made for him, is that these gifts were found in him. If he could give rest and peace, then he could give our life the ultimate affirmation it craves. Our eyes would be forced to look beyond him to discover the source of his power. Only a life totally affirmed can reveal the source of ultimate affirmation. Only a life totally loved can reveal the giver of perfect love. Only a life fully free can finally be the source of our freedom. If rest and peace can come from Jesus of Nazareth, then he must be uniquely related to the eternal source of life, the power of love, and the ground of being. To be in touch with this is to be a part of all that I mean when I say "God."

Perhaps our secular age might look again at this Jesus. Behind the symbols men and women have used to capture him, there was a life at rest, biblical rest, being completely what he was created to be and freeing those around him to be what they were created to be. Here was a life calling others with the power of his love into a new acceptance of their humanity.

He was also a man at peace. Peace was seen in his ability to cross every frontier, to embrace any reality, including death. When we look at his infinite capacity to give himself away, his total lack of defensiveness, his ability to move even into those experiences we regard as life-denying, his freedom to live and to die, there we see peace. Jesus was a life at rest, a life in peace, a life that was secure, affirmed, free, whole.

If we can touch this power, participate in this love, then we can discover new dimensions to our humanity. Standing inside this experience we can begin to see this Jesus with startling freshness. Here we grasp the meaning that Christians in previous generations saw when they called him Saviour, Christ, Reconciler.

10

Loneliness and Destiny

HE WAS lonely. He lived out a destiny. These are our words, and yet they are true to the biblical account that described Jesus of Nazareth two thousand years ago. As such they help to open the curtain that hides him from our understanding, making it possible to embrace him as Lord and Christ in this secular, religionless age. So look now with biblical eyes at his loneliness and at his sense of destiny.

The Bible portrayed a Jesus who was possessed by a purpose that literally consumed him. That purpose was to reveal the life-giving power of love—a revelation that had to come at an exact time and under exact circumstances or it would not be grasped. It had to be the grand finale of his life, and it had to be acted out in Jerusalem. The hand of destiny gripped him tightly. Jerusalem drew him ineluctably. We find a constant reference in his life to the purpose and the time for which he was born. "For this cause came I forth" (Mark 1:38), he said. At the wedding feast in Cana of Galilee, he rebuked his mother for pressing him to be a miracle worker: "My hour has not come," he asserted (John 2:4ff). Later he refused to appear in Jerusalem prematurely, even at his brothers' urging (John 7:8). "Go to the festival yourselves," he said. "I

am not going to Jerusalem because the right time for me
has not come." He stated that a prophet could not die
outside Jerusalem (Luke 13:33), so, when the moment did
arrive, he set his face steadfastly toward the city that held
the key to his destiny and that drew him like a magnet
(Luke 9:51). He did not waver or deviate. Finally, in the
garden of Gethsemane he proclaimed "The time is at
hand for all things to be accomplished" (Luke 21:8); and
his dying words were "It is finished!" (John 19:30). He
was a possessed man, a man with a destiny, compelled to
live out his vision.

Yet in the grip of his destiny he was free! For it was a
destiny he chose, a destiny in which he was fulfilled, a
destiny through which he gave of himself to the world.
Had he turned aside from his purpose, refused his cross,
exhibited cowering fear, his freedom would have been
compromised and his destiny would have been destroyed.

But he discovered—as all people driven by a destiny
discover—that freedom is not free. The inevitable price
of freedom is loneliness, dreadful loneliness. Jesus exhibited the loneliness of one who knows where he is going,
but who is surrounded by those upon whom he yearns to
depend. Yet he sees that they cannot accept or understand his purpose, his meaning, his life.

I see this loneliness in Jesus when the disciples are de-
bating which of them is the greatest. He placed a child in
their midst and said, "Ye must become as little children,"
and still they argued (Matt. 18:1ff). I see his loneliness
when he asked who they thought he was. They responded, "You are the Christ of God," and then they proceeded to tell him what kind of Christ he had to be for their
sakes; and he said, "Get thee behind me, Satan" (Mark
8:27ff). I see his loneliness when he sought to feed the
multitude, and they decided, therefore, to make him their

king, forcing him to escape out of their midst (John 6:15). I see his loneliness in the Palm Sunday procession when the crowds shouted "Hosannah!" to a king (Luke 19:38). No one seemed to realize that the only throne from whence this man would reign would be a cross; the only glory he would possess would be in his death. I see his loneliness in Gethsemane when he went out to pray. His disciples went to sleep, and he said, "Could ye not watch one brief hour?" (Mark 14:37).

Loneliness. Dreadful loneliness. The loneliness of being who you are in a world that does not understand.

Yet the beauty of this free man lay in the fact that he was not at the mercy of his loneliness. He did not grasp at the fulfillment of approval. He did not compromise his integrity for the cheap price of popularity.

A free person does not need to be affirmed by anyone. Affirmation comes in knowing who one is, being at one with the real self, and consequently touching that which is transcendent and eternal. Here we begin to understand what Jesus meant when he said, "I am not alone, for the Father is with me" (John 16:32). This was not religious piety. This was the existential power of the radically free man.

Here was a man possessed by a destiny, choosing freely to live that destiny out, never turning away from his purpose, enduring the loneliness of being and yet never distorted by it. Here was a life revealing the very deep truth that a person in touch with the self can bear any loneliness. A person consciously living out a purpose can dare to walk apart from the crowd, to turn the back on the roar of approval as well as the din of criticism. A free person can chart a course, aim at a goal, walk to a destiny. The world will stand aside for that one, but he or she will ofttimes walk alone.

Jesus knew who he was. He possessed the freedom and the courage to be.

People who know who they are, are free to be what they shall be. Such people can walk steadfastly toward their destiny, toward the Jerusalem moment of truth, where they are fully revealed. Such people know how to choose, how to avoid those activities that dissipate their strength and blur their vision. They know how to cling to those moments that lead to the goal of the realized self—full, free, and capable of living. They know how to escape the guilt that plagues an uncertain person who wonders and worries every time a decision is made lest it be made wrongly. They know how to make loneliness positive instead of negative.

This was the power of Jesus of Nazareth that excited, attracted, and compelled a response. This power lay behind the words with which the first century sought to communicate this life.

The secular, modern spirit can make contact with this Jesus, for we seek the very quality of life he possessed. We have life only when we are grasped by a purpose. We need a vision, a destiny to call our deepest self into reality. We only exist until we know ourselves and chart our path, discover our Jerusalem where we are revealed, and set our faces steadfastly to walk in that direction. Without a clear vision of our Jerusalem beckoning us, we stumble and stagger from one ego trip to another. We experience the despair of our humanity. Lacking the security of being, we search for status, for the approving word, the moment in the sun, always afraid to bear the loneliness that marks the person of destiny who marches to the beat of a drummer that no one else seems to hear.

This loneliness of being was the mark of the one who was called the Christ. It will, therefore, be the mark of a

Christian. When understood it is a welcomed privilege and not a dreaded specter.

Imitate the Christ, then, we are told. That does not mean trying to be "little Jesuses" or seeking to become just like the Christ. That leads only to legalism, to life-killing, religious piety. To imitate Christ means rather that as Jesus became all that he was capable of being, so we—touched by his life, called into his power—seek to become all that we are capable of being. Discipleship involves daring to be free, daring to dream, to fasten onto that which is our Jerusalem, allowing it to draw us down that lonely path to itself. We discover in the process that as our Jerusalem draws us to itself, it also draws us to ourselves. We begin to live: accepting ourselves, loving ourselves, and being ourselves. We begin to know our depths and to realize that we are not alone, for the source of life, the ground of being, the holy God is with us. In this power we can live, love, rejoice, and care as we never dreamed possible before. Standing here we listen to Jesus anew, and begin to appreciate how it was that two thousand years ago men and women could not write of him without calling him the Christ of God.

11

❖

If the Son Shall Set You Free

H E W A S free.

This freedom he promised to his disciples. "If the son has made you free then you are free indeed" (John 8:36).

We look now at his freedom and how he sought to share that freedom with all of the world.

In the seventies a very unusual book topped the fiction best-seller list in America. It was radically different from the volumes that usually occupy that position. It was not a lurid tale of sex in suburbia. It was not a romantic, political, spy, or war story—not even a great historical novel. The cinema industry was challenged to reproduce this story on film. Yet there it stood, popular beyond measure. The rights to bring this book out in paperback were sold for over one million dollars. In this best-selling volume, there were only forty-two pages of printed words. On the surface it was an almost childlike story about a bird.

His name was Jonathan Livingston Seagull.

When such a story sells hundreds of thousands of copies, then we may be sure that the book touches a human nerve, exposes a new dimension of life, and enables its readers to identify their own deep yearnings with the content of the story. When the dedication read "to the real Jonathan Seagull who lives within us all," its hidden power was openly broadcast. The story was a parable, a parable about life and limits, freedom and bondage, love, and—even though the word is never used—it was also, I believe, a parable about the Christ. At least it opened a new angle of vision from which to look at Jesus of Nazareth.

Jonathan Livingston Seagull was a very unusual bird. The other seagulls bothered to learn only the simple routines of life. They flew from shore to food and back to shore. Flying for them was but a means toward the end of satisfying their hunger. But Jonathan rebelled at such habits. He wanted to press the edges of his limits; to explore his power. He exalted in every newfound ability. He tested his endurance. He refused to believe that the gift of flying was for the sole purpose of gaining food. The gift of flying to him was for the purpose of flying, for every moment had its own value. The more he extended the arenas of his experience, the more vibrantly alive he became. He trembled with delight at each joy, at each discovery of pure beauty. He did not accept the conventional limits prescribed for him by the laws of the flock. Naively he thought his fellow seagulls would be ecstatic to hear of his breakthroughs and to learn that they, too, could be free. But he discovered that freedom frightened more lives than it excited, and ofttimes the security of the flock was far more satisfying than the freedom to soar. Thus Jonathan Seagull, instead of being acclaimed for charting new frontiers, was made an outcast. The wondrous insight that he wanted to share became his gift in solitude.

Off he soared, alone, to new horizons, savoring every new discovery, tasting every new sweetness, and finding a world that was wider and deeper than even he had imagined. Finally, Jonathan crossed the limits of death and time and space, but even there his mind continued to confront and break barriers. In his effort to achieve a perfect speed in flying, he found that no number measured perfection; numbers only measure limitations. Perfect speed was not going there, it was being there. The gulls who scorned perfection in favor of travel went nowhere and they went slowly, he observed. Heaven was entered, he determined, not by trying to get there but by knowing that one had already arrived. Life's secret was found when one knew that one's truest nature lived everywhere at once. Life was discovered in the realm of being, not doing; real life crossed time and space and was without limit of tradition or expectation. When Jonathan Seagull realized this, he felt at once a great shock of electric joy; for to see it was to be it.

Jonathan could not, however, be totally free of enslaving limitations without yearning to share that freedom. But how could he show those who had never looked up what it is like to soar a thousand miles beyond the usual limits of life? One is free, he discovered, to go where one wishes to go and to be what one can be, but not if life is lived in bondage to insecurities, fears, or to a life-style that is safe or traditional. If one talks about freedom to those who refuse to be free, those words are inevitably heard as judgment. If visions are related to those who do not dare to dream, the one who has the vision is dismissed as wild, impractical, perhaps even mad or demon-possessed. If one, in obedience to a larger view, lives out a new style of life among those who only do the expected thing, that one might expect to be banished, rejected, and perhaps even killed lest the populace be corrupted.

The deepest law in the whole creation is that human life is made to be free; our destiny, our purpose is to be what we are meant to be. But the life we know is blocked, thwarted, shackled, insecure. We create structure, rituals, superstitions, conventional wisdom to protect our lives. We sacrifice freedom for order and security. We fail to realize that the things that ultimately limit our being are always internal, never external. Those who are free are frightening, for they force us to stop hiding and to look deeply into ourselves. The presence of freedom makes some people so angry at their own lack of freedom that their hatred will destroy their vision, and they will attempt to crucify the bringer of freedom. Others will rid themselves of the threat by falling back in adoration before the bringer of freedom, believing this quality to be divine and therefore beyond the grasp of an ordinary mortal. Since they themselves are not divine this becomes their excuse not to fly, their justification for refusing to dream.

Only those who are touched by freedom—those who, through its power, are turned on to all that life is—only they will know that freedom, limitless humanity, is but the fullness of life. A free person thus reveals the secret of life, the being of this person reflects the ground of being. In such a person life and death, time and space, humanity and divinity—all are seen as self-imposed limits that box people in, distort their vision, and enslave their being.

Yet Jonathan Seagull—free to live, to love, to fly, to dream, to soar to the edges of life where the limits disappear—inevitably turned his attention to the one task that the free life of love cannot avoid. He must introduce other seagulls to this freedom. He did not do this with words or exhortations or with lectures. He did not resort to mighty deeds that others with limited comprehension would only describe as nonhuman miracles. He did it, rather, by living out the meaning of freedom and letting it exert its powerful attraction. He did it by loving the real person who lived underneath the scared person who hated, or underneath the limited person who expressed prejudice, or underneath the enslaved person who moved either to worship or to kill. He did it by allowing the bitterness and the rejection of frightened lives to go unanswered, so that love was not blocked and lives could be free to respond.

This life reflected an immense appeal—even a Godlike appeal. It was inevitable that such a life would draw people to itself even when portrayed symbolically as a seagull.

Through the symbol of a seagull, it is impossible for me not to see Jesus of Nazareth anew: to see beyond the description given him in human words; to see the meaning of his promised gift of freedom; to view afresh the magnetic power of his life. In Jesus I see transfigured beauty, the limitless being of one who pressed the edges of humanity and touched the levers of vital power, crossing every frontier of time and space and life and death. His was a life that opened the doors to freedom, love, and power to those around him. His was a life given away so extravagantly that it inspired Paul to write the self-emptying passage in Philippians (2:5–11) that concludes with the doxology that "at the name of Jesus every knee shall bow." His was a life people saw in the luminous glow of transfiguration. Not surprisingly, this was the life that human beings destroyed to avoid seeing that they lived in slavery. And even as they destroyed him they discovered that he loved the real person underneath the enslaved person who cried for his execution. This was a life so rare, so bold, so free, so full, so alive, so electric, so contagiously attractive that to explain its power people had to use words like *Son of God, Saviour, Lord!*

When this power touches our lives we too are turned on to life's meaning. We are freed to push life's frontiers back until the created purpose of life has been seen, allowing us the courage to be what we can be. Inside this freedom we look again at Jesus of Nazareth and our response is worship. It is not, however, the kind of worship that calls us to recognize our dependency, our sinfulness, or our worthlessness—as worship has so often done in the past. Rather, it is worship that calls us to expand our life and break our limits, enabling us to live and love and share. We might even say that we have been born again. Born free. Born to live in the power of the life of Jesus of Nazareth. We join the new creation (II Cor. 5:17) for "if the Son has set us free, then we are free indeed" (John 8:36).

12

❧

I Am Resurrection—
I Am Life!

"I A M the resurrection, and the life; he who believes in me, though he die, yet shall he live. Do you believe this?" (John 11:25ff).

In many ways the Fourth Gospel frightens me. Its depth challenges my scholarship. Its insight baffles my rationalism. Its profundity threatens to reveal my shallowness. I avoid it. I am willing only to nibble at its edges. I am aware that great scholars like William Temple, C. H. Dodd, and Sir Edwin Hoskyns gave their lives to a study of this book, while I am afraid to approach it. Yet frightening though it be, I cannot ignore it, for it intrigues me. It fascinates me. It calls me. I do not look to the Fourth Gospel for historic accuracy. No life of Jesus can be constructed from this volume. Few if any direct quotations of Jesus can be found here. But no one, I am convinced, understood the deep inner meaning of Jesus of Nazareth better than did the author of the Fourth Gospel.

With carefully chosen words and highly developed theological symbols, the writer of this book interprets this life. For John, he was not the Jesus of history, he was the

Christ of meditation. He was the starkly blinding revelation of life, love, and being. Yet he was fully human. There was no Johannine attempt to prove his divinity, no virgin birth mythology is found here. In and through this historic human life something beyond life was always seen by John. The Fourth Gospel portrayed this beyond, this life-power, as if it were completely historic. This was the secret meaning of Jesus. "In him was life," says the Johannine prologue, "and his life was the light of men."

The Fourth Gospel revealed the Christ figure under a series of symbolic sayings, all of which began with the words *I am: I am* the bread of life. *I am* the living water. *I am* the light of the world. *I am* the good shepherd. *I am* the vine. *I am* the resurrection and the life.

I doubt if the historic Jesus ever actually said any of these things, but the author of this book, meditating on the result of Jesus' life, could not refrain from making these ultimate claims for him. For in this Jesus, John had found Christpower—that is, Jesus became the vine for him because he found him to be the sustainer of life. He became light because in him darkness was vanquished, or living water because in him was found the essence of outgoing caring. This Christpower the author of the Fourth Gospel found in the one historic life—the human being, Jesus of Nazareth.

The Fourth Gospel's story was a meditation on this power and thus it was not an historic account but an interpretation of the life of Jesus of Nazareth. In order to appreciate it, one must be turned on to the life that was in Jesus, set free by the love that was in him, made whole by the power that was in him. An unconverted life could never understand. An uncommitted life could never comprehend. The Fourth Gospel frightens me, it judges my life, it questions my love, it challenges my faith, it reveals my depths and my lack of depth. Yet it is a compelling volume.

The key to this book, I believe, is our ability to distinguish between Jesus and Christ. They are not the same. Jesus was a person; Christ is a title, a theological principle. Jesus was of history; Christ is beyond history. Jesus was human, finite, limited; Christ is power that is divine, infinite, unlimited. Jesus had a mother and a father, an ancestry, a human heritage. He was born. He died. Christ is a principle beyond the capacity of the mind to embrace or human origins to explain. The name of our Lord was not Jesus Christ, as so many of us suppose. He was Jesus of Nazareth about whom people made the startling and revolutionary claim: "You are the Christ."

The simplistic suggestion that Jesus is God is nowhere made in the biblical story. Nowhere! But time after time in historic episode after historic episode, the claim has been made that through Jesus God was revealed—fully, completely, totally.

And who is God? God is not a figure in the sky who thinks and acts, who feels and directs. God is the source of life. God is seen wherever life is lived, and God is not alien or separated from that life. God is the source of love. God is seen wherever love is shared, and God is not alien or separated from that love. God is the ground of being. God is seen wherever one has the courage to be, and God is not alien or separated from that being.

In Jesus of Nazareth men and women saw the fullness of life being lived, the depth of love being shared, the courage to be revealed. To them Jesus made known the meaning of life and love and being. He revealed God, and whenever God is seen in human life, that power is called Christ. "You are the Christ, Jesus"—that was the claim. "You are the Christ, for in your life we have seen

the meaning of all life. In your love we have seen the
meaning of all love. In your being we have seen the
ground of all being."

That was the Christ that John saw in Jesus of
Nazareth.

To be in this Christ is to come alive. It is to dare to
love, to dare to be. It is to escape the bondage of our
selves and to fly. It is to press the limits of our humanity,
to meet another life openly, honestly, to touch and to
share. It is to escape our estrangement. In these moments
we know that this power is bigger than death, for it is
bigger than life. This is Christpower. This was the meaning of the historic human being known as Jesus of Nazareth. This was why the biblical writers, and even we today, have to use the language of myth and parable to
explain him. This was what lay behind every miracle account of the biblical story. This was the meaning of the
virgin birth accounts of Matthew and Luke, and this was
the secret behind every "I am" claim of the Fourth Gospel. In the Fourth Gospel it was not the Jesus of history
who spoke, it was the Christpower, eternal and divine,
which people had experienced in Jesus who was made to
utter words through the mouth of this historic life. That
is the interpretive clue to the profound meditation we call
the Gospel of John.

Take this now, if you will, to the episode of the raising of Lazarus in chapter 11 of John's story, for here was
the Fourth Gospel's account of what happened when this
Christpower confronted death. The scene was the village
of Bethany. The deceased was a close friend. Jesus had
been a guest in his home. The mourners gathered. The
burial was complete. The cave was sealed. Jesus himself,
arriving late, was caught in the emotions of bereavement.
He wept. His humanity was real. Then a strange dialogue

ensued with Martha, the sister of the departed Lazarus:

"Master, if you had been here my brother would not have died."

"Martha, your brother will live again."

"Lord, don't play pious religious games with me. Don't give me cliché assurances. I know he will live again at the general resurrection at the last day. Don't preach to me! I believe in life after death. That is not my problem. My problem is *now:* grief, bereavement, loneliness, loss, hurt, pain. Speak to my life *now,* Lord."

"Martha, listen to my being, not my doing. I am resurrection. I am life. If you are touched by me, even though you die, you will live. If you are inside my power, you will never die. Human life is not eternal, Martha. Human life is like grass, and as the prophet says, grass perishes, flowers fade (Isa. 40:8). But the Word of God, the logos, the Christpower, will never pass away. I can make you live, Martha, now and forever; for human life touched by Christpower will transcend every limit. It will share in eternity. Do you believe this, Martha? Do you believe that I can give you resurrection and life?"

"Yes, Lord," Martha answered, "I believe that you are the Christ. I believe that God's life, God's love, God's being are breaking into human history through your life. I believe that in you time stands still."

So in this episode the Christpower in Jesus of Nazareth confronted death, and death was seen to yield before it, for death was a denial of life. Death's apparent victory was reversed. Its sting was lost. For Jesus brought life. He brought the power of Christ.

John continued to ponder this narrative and again he heard the power of Christ speak:

"Lazarus, come forth," he had Jesus say. Death yielded. Lazarus came. He lived. Those who believed saw in this the glory of God, for the glory of God is nothing other than life lived, restored, made whole, forgiven, resurrected. It is life that has been invited into the timelessness of love.

The story of Lazarus was not a literal story. It was the truth arrived at by the author of the Fourth Gospel after long years of meditating on the power in the life of Jesus of Nazareth. His meditation focused in this instance, I believe, on the parable of Lazarus and Dives (Luke 16:20ff), a parable that he related as if it were an historic episode. But regardless of whether it was a literal story, it is truth—deep, profound truth. For I am convinced that life, not death, is finally real.

Why am I convinced? Because I have seen people resurrected by love. I have seen new radiance, new hope, new life, new love break into human existence. I have seen death conquered in more than one life. I have watched beauty transcend ugliness, love overcome hatred, life overwhelm death. I have seen faith transform fear. I have watched life, love, and being revealed in specific history. There is power whenever eternity touches time with the gift of love and calls us to live. That is what the Bible means by the title Christ—living, eternal, God-given power breaking into human life. It is not alien or foreign in our world. This is the power that was seen in Jesus of Nazareth, and so people called him *the* Christ. He revealed the meaning of God, the nature of God, by living, loving, being.

So John had Jesus say: "I am resurrection. I am life." Our world yearns to know this Christ; to find joy in a new commitment; to become new creatures; to shed our fears, our fantasies, our need for status symbols, our prejudices. The pathway to such a life, however, lies in opening ourselves to all that Christpower means. We must

dare to love and dare to live. We must learn to give ourselves away freely. Waste love. Grasp life. Let our being
reflect the power that sets us free. We *are* loved, we *are*
accepted, we *are* forgiven. *That* is the meaning of Christ.
All we must do is be open to it, accept that love, accept
that acceptance, accept that forgiveness, and watch it roll
back the curtains hiding our lives from ourselves. We will
watch the stage on which our life is being lived expand so
that even the final curtain of death seems not so drastic,
not so powerful. When we live open to this Christ, we
will know the deepest secret of life. Christpower will hold
us in life. We will die, but in this Christ we are touched
by a love that will not die, and that love will hold our
mortal lives in the hand of that which is immortal.

"I am the resurrection and the life. He who believes
in me, though he dies, yet shall he live. Do you believe
this, Martha?" Once we get inside the Christian experience, we can join with Martha and say: "Yes, Lord, I believe you are the Christ, for you have given me the gift
of life."

13

❖

I Am Light

"I A M the light of the world. He who follows me will not walk in darkness" (John 8:12).

In some of the interior caverns of the mountains in the western part of Virginia, one can experience the phenomenon of almost absolute darkness; a darkness so intense that even our hand before our face is not visible. It is a clinging, devastating, fearful feeling! Such darkness affects more than just the sense of sight; it is experienced as deathly silence, even as frightening pain. It makes us realize how little true darkness we ever know in our electrified, bustling, modern world.

To the ancient ancestors of the human race, each night brought with it something of the same terror created by these interior caverns. There were no street lights, candlelight, or neon signs—nothing but darkness—a darkness that our primitive forbears could not dispel. Only the sun and the moon and the stars could hurl back this fearful, enveloping presence. When ancient people first discovered how to use fire, they were quite convinced that they had captured part of the power of the sun or the moon. It had come to them as a gift from the gods of light, arriving on earth via the crackling lightning. Not surprisingly, whatever dispelled darkness became the object of ancient worship. The sun, the moon, the stars, and fire all occupy important chapters in human religious development—all have been worshiped as gods and, indeed, all still play a role in our contemporary worship.

It is not an accident that today fire is still placed on our altars to begin worship, as the candles are lit. It is not an accident that today the setting sun is an analogy by which death is understood, as our evening hymns proclaim; or that the rising sun is an analogy of resurrection, as our Easter and morning hymns proclaim. Even the popularity of astrology charts indicates that many of us still believe our lives are controlled by the moon and stars. The symbols of light and darkness are familiar concepts in the traditional language of our religious heritage. They have been since the dawn of time.

When we examine the biblical story we meet the symbols of light and darkness again and again. When the gospel writers wrote of the birth of Jesus, they spoke of a powerful light splitting the darkness of night (Luke 2:9; Matt. 2:9). When they portrayed the death of Jesus, they spoke of darkness being over the whole land from the sixth hour until the ninth hour (Luke 23:44).

When Judas went out to betray the Christ, John's Gospel notes that "it was night" (John 13:30). When early Christians spoke of hell, the ultimate loneliness, they called it "outer darkness" (Matt. 8:12). When Saul met his Lord on the Damascus road, he was blinded by light (Acts 9:3). When Matthew used the words of a prophet to interpret Jesus, he wrote, "The people who sat in darkness have seen the great light" (Matt. 4:16). Finally Jesus himself in the language of the Fourth Gospel is pictured as saying, "I am light—the light of the world" (John 8:12).

In our search for another symbolic clue or insight into the person of Jesus of Nazareth, we look now for the inner meaning of the word "light" and its contrast "darkness" as these words were used in the biblical story.

In the first century, people believed that this world was under the domination of a demonic power of darkness that warred against God's purpose in creation. This demonic power was seen in both mental and physical illnesses. Mentally sick people were thought to be demon-possessed (Luke 8:26ff). Physical fever represented a demonic power that had to be broken (Luke 4:39). Chronic diseases were manifestations of being bound by Satan (Luke 13:16). All sickness was the result of demonic power. This was a common, universally held understanding, and the word darkness stood for this. This darkness was personified and called the "Prince of Darkness." In the mind of the first century, this satanic figure ruled the world.

In a literal, surface way this represented a prescientific superstition. But before we dismiss it on that basis, look for a moment underneath the literalism to the reality they sought to explain and the truth to which they were pointing. They were saying that the world was made for something more glorious than it was achieving. They were denying, even in the face of evidence to the contrary, that sickness was intended to be the destiny of life. They were asserting that no human life was created for physical or mental distortions. They were recognizing that whenever life failed to achieve its potential, its fullness, its glory, it revealed a corruption of creation, or in their words "a fall into sin." This they called darkness. It enslaved them, victimized them, and they were almost powerless to escape its grasp.

This view of life lay behind the Jewish passion to obey

the Law. The Law, they believed, was a guide to the fullness of life. If only one Jew could obey the Law—every
jot and tittle—the demonic power would be broken. Life
could then be free and whole, and the world would see
what it meant to be true children of God. Only in this
way, they believed, could the Prince of Darkness be dispelled. With all their might, the devout people of Israel
sought to achieve this perfection; but tragically, the hard-
er they tried, the more they failed. The final results of
their efforts were not fulfilled persons, but the self-righ-
teous: proud, arrogant, unloving, insensitive, unfeeling,
uncaring. Such people were, in Jesus' words, whitewashed
sepulchres—shiny outside but dead inside (Matt. 23:27).
In their despair, the Hebrew people faced the fact that
there was no escape from this power that distorted life, at
least no escape that they could achieve.

Still these Hebrews steadfastly refused to lower their
eyes, to deny their dreams. They would not accept what
was, as if that were what should be. They believed life
pointed to a glory they could not achieve. This was the
profound insight hiding underneath their symbols. No
other words captured their meaning so well as "the world
is under the power of darkness." They insisted that some
demonic power was twisting, warping, and ruling human
life, usurping the place of God in history and causing
men and women to walk in darkness. It was the darkness
experienced when people pretended to be what they knew
they were not. It was the darkness of repression, the inability to face—much less love—one's true self. It was the
darkness of living in fear that life would be revealed, exposed, found wanting, destroyed. The Hebrew mind saw
human life on this deep level. Hence they wrote that all
life walks in darkness.

This was the darkness into which Jesus of Nazareth

was born, and against which he was interpreted. Because of what people experienced in him they called him the "Prince of Light." In this Jesus they found a life whose power of love could dispel darkness (John 1:5), banish demons (Luke 9:37ff), heal sickness (Mark 1:40ff), restore life (Luke 7:11ff), and recall men and women to a new creation (John 21:15ff). They found this life to be one that could meet guilt with forgiveness (Luke 23:34), hatred with love (Mark 15:29ff), fear with acceptance (Mark 14:41, 42). They saw in him a portrait of what life was created to be: free, whole, giving, loving. Yet the conflict between his light and the world's darkness was not simple or easy, for inevitably many preferred the security of a darkness that was familiar to the wrenching reordering of life that light required. So people "in their darkness" rejected, abused, arrested, tried, convicted, and executed the bringer of light. When this man died, the inner vision of those who had glimpsed his power could see only an all-enveloping darkness that prevailed, at least momentarily, over the whole land. The Prince of Darkness reigned supreme.

However, the story did not end there, the Christian witness asserted. After that darkness there came the eternal dawn (Mark 16:1ff). Love restored life, and that life broke the power of darkness forever. Thus John could write: "In him was life, and his life was the light of men and women, and his life shines in darkness, and the darkness cannot extinguish it" (1:4, 5). This is the Christian story told under the symbols of darkness and light, the most ancient religious symbols of human experience. It was a story, a faith, that proclaimed that love had the power to banish distortion, that love enabled life to be what it was created to be. Love restored life to its true purpose. This love was not an abstract theory, they believed, but rather was known in a concrete, historic life: "I am the light of the world. He who follows me will not walk in darkness but will have the light of life" (John 8:12). Light was revealed when love touched them and enabled them to grasp their humanity, fulfill their potential, live out their destiny as full, free, loving people.

To be in the power of this Jesus was thus to discover the depths of life and being. It was to be set free from fear to discover the courage to live and to love. This was why Christians were called "children of light (Eph. 5:8)." The gospel written under these ancient religious symbols was saying that we walk in light when we grasp our human destiny, celebrate our human grandeur, achieve our human potential. We become light-bearers when we stand on the battle lines of our world wherever humanity is threatened, wherever justice is thwarted and life is tested. However, ours is a reflected light, reflected from the one who was seen as the source of light, whose power transformed life, whose light illumined the world, whose love restored creation.

The gospel message was thus a call to let the light of our full, restored humanity shine in the darkness of this world. It was a call to be our deepest, truest selves, so that people might see in us the meaning of life and be drawn through us to worship the source of our light. It was a call to labor without ceasing, without despair, without defeat, to share the gift of life, the heritage of humanity, the fullness of justice with every child of God. Light must shine to be seen. Light must have an empowering source before it can shine. People found that light in Jesus of Nazareth, and they were drawn to him. We translate their symbols, probe their words, and see their meaning. Wonder of wonders! That meaning still translates in the twentieth century.

14

❧

I Am Bread

"I A M the bread of life; he who comes to me shall not hunger" (John 6:35).

I think it safe to say that the eating of food is at one and the same time both the most commonplace and the most profound experience of any life. It is a physical, emotional, psychological, and spiritual phenomenon, whether it is realized or not. The first moment in which love is experienced by any human being is the moment when he or she first is fed. Newborn babies enter life separate and alone. The vast new world is filled with unknown stimuli; but when children are fed by their mothers, they are held, cradled, and rocked. They know warmth, security, caring. It is all but impossible for an infant to receive food without feeling community and love. So it is that, deep in our unconscious minds, food becomes associated with something far deeper than food. It is a symbol for love; never are the two separated.

When people eat together, they build community by sharing life. Food is always symbolic as well as physical. The birthday cake at any age and with any number of candles marks the recipient as special, queen or king for a day. The mug of coffee with a midmorning caller, the cup of tea served a midafternoon guest, the cocktail be-the evening meal, or the nightcap in late evening with a friend: all of these are symbols of life, love, and relationship. No friendship ever grows unless meals are eaten together. Even our eating prohibitions rising out of the racial and religious bigotry of the past reveal that eating was a social, community-building, life-giving experience. When death is experienced and grief mutes our words, we go to the home of the bereaved carrying a nonverbal message of love. It is always food. Even the snack that a child eats when he or she returns home from school serves a far deeper purpose than the relieving of hunger. It is a symbol of belonging, of being back in the nest. It celebrates security. The child is home.

This deeper meaning of food is seen when psychiatrists identify a number of emotional problems in life as "oral neuroses." Obesity is not just a physical problem; it has a psychological dimension as well. People do take in orally to compensate for the love they lack, to overcome their loneliness, for food is a love-substitute. Human life searches orally for pleasure and meaning, not unlike children who explore everything by mouth.

Alcoholism also has its oral dimension. Alcoholics drink to escape frustration, defeat, a feeling of inadequacy. They too are searching with their mouths for the love and security they once knew as infants. The habit of smoking likewise appears to psychiatrists to be a mild form of an oral neurosis, an attempt to recapture the pleasure and warmth of nursing. Cigarettes, cigars, and pipes are really nothing but adult thumb-sucking, adult pacifiers, pseudo-food, love substitutes.

The more one probes the psychological meaning of food, the more profound one sees the experience of eating to be. Indeed, to know the quality of life in any family, one can simply analyze the eating habits of its members.

To see the profound effect eating has in the human experience, we have only to look at how the vocabulary of food has shaped the very meaning and content of the English language: A person of good aesthetic judgment is said to have "good taste"; one speaks of "feeding" egos and "swallowing" pride; about "digesting" reports and ideas. A job or vocation becomes the way one earns "bread and butter." We speak of getting our "teeth" into some program or project, or even of being "chewed out" by some authority figure.

A touchy issue is called a "hot potato"; an unmerited bonus or an unexpected joy becomes "gravy." A person is described as "cool as a cucumber," "nutty as a fruitcake," "as American as apple pie," and as "boiling mad" (which brings the suggestion to "simmer down"). One speaks of "stewing in our own juices" or "cooking our goose." Perhaps the most telling phrase comes when one who is good and generous is described as possessing the "milk of human kindness."

Eating food is a profound human experience. It is physical, emotional, psychological, and spiritual. Only in reaching this level of understanding will the meaning the Fourth Gospel found in Jesus the Christ ever be comprehended. This writer recorded Jesus as saying: "I am the bread of life."

This author knew that bread—food, eating—was a symbol for love. As bread physically fills a body, so love psychologically fills a life. The Christ claim to be the bread of life was thus a claim to be the power that fulfills the deepest needs of human life. Those needs do not change from age to age or with the passage of time. All life is lonely, separate, insecure. All life hungers and thirsts for wholeness, for being. All life seeks that elusive something that satisfies, but somehow no life seems to find it.

It is not found in wealth; one has only to ask the lonely wealthy person to discover that. It is not found in social prestige or importance; one can ask the social pacesetters of any city and they will verify this. It is not found in achieving power; one can ask the people whose decisions govern our nation, our state, and our city. It is not found in seeking escape from life's tensions; one has only to ask those who own a boat, a holiday haven, a mountain retreat, and they will be eloquent witnesses that these do not finally satisfy.

Life hungers for that food that does not pass away— the affirmation of our being, the power of love, the *bread of life.*

This was the meaning the Fourth Gospel found in Jesus, so John's Jesus could say: "I am the bread of life. He who comes to me will never hunger."

In these words perhaps one can begin to perceive this Christ, even though this is a rationalistic, nonreligious age. Every life knows its deepest hunger, its infinite need to be fed. It is essential, however, that this Christpower not be a mirage, an absurd dream created by that human need. We crave a living Lord, we will not accept an illusion; we require a fact, we will not be deluded by a fiction. We search for the true meaning of this Christ though that search causes the barriers of our imagination to be broken so that even the searcher must blink at the magnitude of the Christ claim.

Confronting us are the mysterious formulas that attempt to prove his divinity. Jesus is surrounded by miraculous accounts of power, accounts that hide him from our secular eyes, and therefore accounts that must boldly be swept aside as we press toward the meaning of that life. For his meaning is not found in the supernatural accretions that encapsulate him. Beneath them we must discover the awesome affirming presence of love or he will not be Christ for this generation.

Love is the power that sets us free to be. Love is that which creates our humanity. Love is the ingredient required if we are to achieve wholeness. Wherever in life we find love in an ultimate sense, there we will find our Saviour. If that love was present in Jesus of Nazareth, then he had a right to claim the saving title. If the power of love seen in him can transcend the generations, then the title *the Christ of God* can rightfully be his. If his love can satisfy the insatiable yearnings of our humanity, then this generation also can call him Lord, for he will not be foreign to our life. His presence will be seen in every experience of life that fulfills, feeds, and sustains. He will thus be the *bread of life* to us.

So look at him! Look not at his divinity; but look, rather, at his freedom. Look not at the exaggerated tales of his power; but look, rather, at his infinite capacity to give himself away. Look not at the first-century mythology that surrounds him; but look, rather, at his courage to be, his ability to live, the contagious quality of his love. Allow yourself to "feast" your eyes on him. "Taste" his power—not in some cannibalistic orgy, not even just in a ritualistic communion service—but "feed" on him by being open to that unique Christpower in him, the same Christpower that is in every free person who has known his love and his affirmation. Stop the frantic search! Be still and know that this is God—this love, this freedom, this life, this being. And when you are accepted, accept yourself; when you are forgiven, forgive yourself; when you are loved, love yourself. Grasp that Christpower, and dare to be yourself!

As you are fed, so learn to feed one another with the living *bread,* the love of life. Then you can hear the power of the Fourth Gospel's claim for Jesus the Christ: "I am the bread of life."

That author wanted us to be sure that we did not miss his point, so in his gospel there was no account of the Last Supper, where Jesus, on the night before the crucifixion, took, blessed, broke, and gave bread to his disciples. The reason for this omission is very clear. In John's mind, the moment Jesus was nailed to the cross was the moment when the *bread of life* was taken, blessed, broken, and given. The power that feeds life so that it never hungers again was seen there on the cross. There love was revealed in the magnificent picture of the free man, giving his life away to the world.

He both makes known and is the source of life. We worship him by living in his freedom, sharing in his being, giving of his love; and we call him Lord, Saviour, for he is *bread—the bread of life.*

PART IV

❧ ❧ ❧

*Return
to the
Center*

15

❧

The Nonreligious Christ

WHO IS Jesus of Nazareth? What does it mean to say of him: "You are the Christ"? How does the power he possessed make contact with us today? These are now our questions.

We have probed the meaning of Jesus in different ways. We have attempted to set him in the context of his Hebrew heritage so that we can see beyond the theological accretions that blind us to his power. We have isolated images from that Hebrew world by which people sought to get an explanatory handle on his life. We have re-created in detail the portrait in the Hebrew scriptures of the Servant figure by which, as we suggested, Jesus came to understand himself. We have examined certain key words used by this Jesus that give insight into his meaning, and certain key words used by a worshiping church to capture the experience they had with him.

My hope has never been to prepare a systematic Christology for a seminary textbook, but rather to bring aspects of his meaning into a shaft of light that comes from looking in a new way, from a new angle, and against a new background. This is an essential task today, not because the traditional approach and old orthodoxies are wrong, but because they are irrelevant. Our world simply can no longer make contact with the thought forms in which the church originally defined its Christ in the early ecumenical councils. To be accused of being a Nestorian,[1] or an Apollinarian,[2] or an Arian[3]—three heresies of the early church—might be serious indeed, but somehow it does not fill our lives with fear and horror. Each of these classical heresies might well be an inadequate theological definition of the Christ figure, but they all represented the human attempt, in the thought forms of that age, to find personal meaning in this Christ. We must be free today to seek as openly as they were able to seek; we must be free to comprehend him within the thought forms of our day. Orthodoxy will have no power unless honest heresy is a possibility. Heresy will be a virtue and not a liability as long as it is offered within the worship of the Christian community and is open to gentle corrections through love from those who have a different perspective, a deeper knowledge, and a wider experience. If the Christian church is to survive, we must encourage our sons and daughters to search in new ways, even to run the risk of nonbelief and heresy. The most disturbing sign on the horizon today is not the eroding of the classical creeds but the fearful critical defensiveness that emanates from those who are self-appointed "defenders of the faith."

If the language of the traditional theological vocabulary is the product of a realm that no longer exists, if the concepts through which our gospel is communicated are no longer translatable, then the task of defining our Christian faith in this generation is incredibly difficult. If being a Christian in the twentieth century demands that I accept a first-century view of genetics and astronomy or a prescientific understanding of miracle, the supernatural, and demon-possession in order to comprehend the Christ figure, then I must either split my mind or be forced to say "no" to the whole Christian enterprise.

If calling Jesus "Lord" means bending our minds into intellectual pretzels, then fewer and fewer people will make commitments to him, for he will make less and less sense. I am not concerned about defending the power or person of Jesus. I trust this book has made that abundantly clear. What does concern me deeply is how that person and that power can be translated in our times. I am concerned about the earthen vessel of our theological understanding in which we try to carry the treasure of our faith.

Rudolf Bultmann, the German Bible scholar, gave the world the word "demythologize." In fundamentalist circles it was and perhaps still is a fearful word. Literal minds heard in it the hint that Christianity was mythical, like Grimm's fairy tales. This was not Bultmann's suggestion. No reputable scholar today seriously doubts that Jesus of Nazareth was a fact of history. But Jesus as fact is always interpreted. Those who interpreted him were creatures of their times who looked at reality through the mind-set and assumptions of their day. There was no perfect objectivity in any of their interpretations.

The lack of objectivity in these interpretations should not be surprising. Four witnesses to the same accident are capable of widely divergent descriptions. Their reporting of any event reveals those forces that shape and form them as individuals. Who they are inevitably colors what their eyes see and their ears hear.

If we take this general subjectivity and add to it the cultural prejudices, the scientific understandings, and the historic perspective of a specific age, we begin to fathom what Bultmann meant by Christian mythology. It is the interpretive framework historically conditioned that surrounded Jesus of Nazareth. This, Bultmann insisted, must be demythologized every generation.

One needs to look no further than the historic creeds[4] to find the glaring need to demythologize. The creeds assumed a three-tiered universe that died with Copernicus. The creedal faith could be paraphrased as follows:

I believe in the God above in the heavenly tier, who created this world on a lower level and sent his son down into it. The son, after his death, descended to the region of hell or of the dead; then he was resurrected back to the earth. In time he ascended to the heavenly sphere from whence he sent the Holy Spirit down to our level to indwell the church through history. Finally, at the culmination of time, we will all be united up in the heavenly region.

In this creedal statement we run the gamut of those three tiers, somewhat like a busy elevator. This framework holding the Christian's primary statement of faith is unbelievable to our twentieth-century, secular minds. It is the mythological language of another age. Unless it is demythologized we should not be surprised when fewer and fewer people take Christianity seriously.

In order to demythologize the Jesus story, we must seek to determine what it was that really occurred as distinct from the way in which it was interpreted. We need to discover what first-century people experienced that compelled them to tell the Jesus story in the appropriate categories of their day. Why did fourth-century people, who gave the creeds their final shape, believe that those particular words accurately expressed the truth of the Christian heritage? Can we get beneath the words, experience what they experienced, and embrace the truth they embraced? Was it real? What was the objective reality?

Can we translate that reality into the mind of the twentieth century? That is the primary task facing every Christian spokesperson today.

In order to begin this undertaking, we need first to review briefly the human situation, which Jesus of Nazareth appeared to meet, that caused people to make the startlingly revolutionary claim for him, "Thou art the Christ."

This human situation was outlined in an earlier chapter where sin was defined as the universal split between what persons know they are and what persons wish they could be. Self-negation was described as the result of the inadequacy of love in human life. Insecurity, a sense of brokenness, and the quest for status were identified as symptoms of the human situation.

In this sense sin, biblically, is a description of our being, not our doing. Human life is locked into self-centeredness, searching constantly for the affirmation that would free it from bondage. Whatever brings affirmation becomes a "saviour," and we will bow in worship before it no matter how bizarre its shape might be. With this in mind, focus now on the story of Jesus to see if that story can be retold in the language and the concepts of our secular generation.

The meaning of Jesus is found where his being made contact with the being of all human life. Hence we look at his freedom to be and at the effect that freedom had on others. We look at his security, his fulfillment, his peace, his capacity to give and love and care. These signs of his being become our interpretive clues. We watch his struggle to share these gifts with others. Then we have an angle of vision that will enable us to understand who he was in a new way and to respond with a new commitment.

The first event of his life described biblically was the moment of birth. The accounts of this moment were beautifully told, full of symbol and wonder (Luke 1, 2; Matt. 1, 2). They were, however, clearly nonhistorical.[5] All birth narratives are legendary. No one waits outside a hospital room, or a home, to greet the birth of a great and important person. Birth narratives tell a great deal about the adult power of a life, but they tell very little about the literal events of the birth.[6] This in no way minimizes the importance of the stories of Jesus' birth. They were profound interpretive accounts in the language of first-century mythology designed to assert that the power present in the life of Jesus of Nazareth was beyond the capacity of human life alone to produce. These narratives were highly stylized, polished, liturgically informed, poetic interpretations of the inner meaning of this historic figure—Jesus, called the Christ—whose life story was to follow. They asserted that Jesus revealed life, love, and being—our deepest symbols for God.

Following the nativity came the Baptism (Matt. 3:1ff, Luke 3:1–11), which stood for that moment when Jesus' conscious mind was invaded by an awareness that the life, love, and being he possessed were of God and must be shared. In the Baptism there was an acceptance of this purpose and this destiny. It was pictorially described in the mythology of the time. The heavens were a dome with a kind of sliding door that opened. (This image of heaven was drawn from the Hebrew heritage, Ezek. 1:1.) The Spirit of God descended like a dove and rested upon him. The words of election were pronounced: "Thou art my beloved son." Jesus realized that his life was unique, that somehow the meaning of God was to be revealed in him and through him, and that he must bear the Messianic function of bringing the meaning and power of that

God to human life. To be Messiah was to be Saviour.
Saviour was to break the power of sin, to love human beings into life, to heal the internal divisions of life, to
bring wholeness.

But to be aware of one's purpose and destiny and to
know how to accomplish that purpose and destiny are two
vastly different things, hence the Baptism was followed by
the temptation (Matt. 4:4–11, Mark 1:12–13, Luke
4:1–13). Once again we must push aside the literal details.
The account, as we have it, dealt with a devil who spoke
in spatial images akin to those in the world of Superman,
where one could go in an instant to a mountain so high
that the glory of all the kingdoms of the world was visible
and then back to the Temple of Jerusalem. All of this
was possible while remaining in a vast wilderness that, although expressed externally, I am convinced existed only
internally. Behind all of that content furnished by the
first century's attempt to interpret was Jesus' inner wres-
tling with the question: "How can I bring the world the
gift of love that fills life full?"

"Shall I be an economic saviour? Shall I turn stones
into bread? Bread does not finally satisfy the deepest
needs of human life. Fulfillment in life does not come
with the satisfaction of physical needs. Food does not give
the freedom to be. Physical fulfillment does not bring life
or wholeness. Human life is not sustained by bread
alone." Thus that possibility was ruled out. An economic
saviour he would not be.

"Shall I be a military saviour? Shall I seek to bring
power, status, and splendor to human life? Shall I bow
down and worship the quest for fulfillment in the symbols
of might and wealth? Shall I have the kingdoms and their
glory to feed the human ego? Shall I seek to convey life's
ultimate meaning by satisfying the insatiable human need

to have importance and value attributed to the individual?" Finally the answer became clear and Jesus responded: "God only is the object of worship. To set any false source of fulfillment where God alone belongs is to worship evil, to pervert life." So deep is our need, so incomplete is our life, that there is not enough status in the world to satisfy any human being. Wholeness does not and cannot lie in human grandeur or glory. There is no security in the transitory realm of human importance. Jesus could not be a saviour who would give status and power.

"Shall I be a religious saviour? Shall I cast myself off the pinnacle of the Temple and demonstrate my religious power? Shall I use religious tricks and take the *things* of worship and make them the *object* of worship? Shall I offer religion as the perfect mask behind which people can hide their insecurities? But that is not real. That is delusional. No religious attitude or religious object, no pious words or pious rituals are the doorway to wholeness. Only the God who is the source of life, the source of love, the ground of being can restore life and being. The whole realm of religion can be a barrier, a hiding place. To follow the Christian Lord is not calculated to make one religious. If that is to be the result, then Christianity has failed. Religion can be one more intolerable form of bondage, one more neurotic way to cover the human feeling of inadequacy. There is no Messianic function performed unless a life is set free, a yoke is broken, wholeness is restored." So this religious temptation was rejected. "God cannot be used," said Jesus. "You shall not tempt the Lord your God." Neither could Jesus be a religious saviour.

Emerging from this inner wilderness, Jesus knew himself to be alive with the life of God, in tune with the love of God, grounded in the being of God. He was aware that the purpose of his life was to share that presence, to bring love, to give life, to make whole, to heal the hurt of unlove, to break the power of sin. Only by doing this could the Messianic task of "overcoming the sin of the world" be accomplished. The problem still remained— How?

Because Jesus understood sin on the level of being, not *doing*, all of the traditional "saviour" roles were inadequate. He could not be a good example that people might install in some ideal category and try to copy. If one seeks fulfillment or wholeness in following a good example, the final result is inevitably the religious bigot who is caught in the slavery of self-righteousness and who finds worth in feeling superior to those who have not achieved such heights of piety. There is no life power found in being compared to an example of goodness. It is rather a symbol of judgment. Those of us who are parents have an excellent opportunity to see this truth. How much of our children's behavior is positively changed when we compare them with each other using such admonitions as "Be like your sister"? The real message is: "You are not good enough. Your sister is better." And this is destructive of life. It is judgmental. Its judgment increases the sense of inadequacy. It drives the victim deeper into his or her shell.

I have a very able and talented younger brother whom I deeply admire. We are both ordained clergy. After I left home to begin studying for the ministry, my brother was asked to deliver the sermon in our church on Youth Sunday. He did so, very ably, prompting a saintly lady to ask him afterward if he intended to "follow in his big brother's footsteps." His response was immediate: "Hell, no, Lady! I'm going to make some of my own." In shock the lady went away muttering that this boy would never make it in the ministry. How wrong she was! She did not realize that holding up an example challenges our sense of self-worth. It does not affirm us. Jesus could not be an "example saviour," for the good example produces only a religion of good works, duty, and finally death.

Nor could Jesus be the "substitute saviour" that so many theories of the atonement seem to suggest. The idea of the "substitute saviour" lies behind the "bloody hymns" so popular in the revival tradition of the eighteenth and nineteenth centuries. Those hymns were obsessed with the shedding of the Saviour's blood. In its crassest form, this substitutionary view of the Messiah's role went like this:

I am a sinner. That is, I have done many bad deeds. I deserve to be punished. God my creator and judge must satisfy the inner sense of divine justice. So I am sentenced to hell to pay for my sins. But when the time comes for the day of reckoning, Jesus takes my place. God allows him to take my punishment for me. He is beaten for me. His blood is shed for me; I am washed in it and made clean. Jesus died for my sins.

Somehow God became a stern ogre more intent on saving face than on giving love or life. How difficult it would be to worship such divine wrath! A god who would crucify Jesus to satisfy an offended sense of justice is no God for our generation. A "substitute saviour" will not translate in our day, if indeed it ever really did.

For Jesus, to be the Messiah meant that he must bring love to the unloved, freedom to the bound, wholeness to the distorted, peace to the insecure. Only in this way could he overcome the sin of the world. The only power that can ultimately save is love, and love was the deepest meaning of Jesus' life.

Love is one of those priceless commodities that cannot be bought, earned, or merited. Love is always a gift. It is grace. Human lives can receive love, and once received, it can be shared. No human life, however, can originate it or create it. Yet no life can finally be human without it. The presence of love lifts us inevitably beyond human life, for love is the meaning of God. The one who can bring this healing, life-giving love perfectly must, finally, be seen as of God. To bring the love that creates wholeness is to be the saviour of humankind. It is to accomplish God's purpose in creation, to fulfill the Messianic task.

All of this Jesus of Nazareth grasped and understood. He knew this gift of infinite love was his to give. He knew, following the temptation episode, what he would not do, what would not work; but the path that he would follow was not yet clear, though the options may have been forming. On this note he began his public career. He accepted the Messianic vocation. He saw as his task the inauguration of the reign of life, love, and being; to recall and restore the whole created order to the fullness and beauty of creation; to open the door that enabled life to be lived by bringing to it the necessary power of the love of God. But how? From the beginning of his public ministry in Nazareth to the Garden of Gethsemane, I think that this was always an open question.

First, he chose to share this freeing gift with the world by talking about it. He announced in Nazareth that in his life the power of love that issued in life was present (Luke 4:21). To know love is to enter the kingdom of God. "It is upon you" (Mark 1:15), he asserted. His parables spelled out the quality of life in the kingdom where wholeness abounded. In the parable of the Good Samaritan, he revealed that love crosses such ego-serving barriers as race and nationality. He indicated that the mark of the kingdom was the gift of self-acceptance and forgiveness, as in the prodigal son who "came to himself" and the waiting father who went out to embrace, to accept, and to forgive (Luke 15:1ff). The kingdom was seen in the publican who, in the act of prayer, had the capacity to look at himself in honesty, admit who he was to his own conscious mind, and know the inner healing that comes when the game of "let's pretend" ceases (Luke 18:9ff). Behind all Jesus' parables, his sayings, his public teaching was his attempt to share his gift of love through words: to talk about it, to invite men and women to listen to it, to respond to it, to be grasped by it.

But his listening audience did not hear. Perhaps they could not hear, for they listened through ears distorted by their insecurity. They heard the words of one who would feed their egos by establishing a new kingdom on earth in whose splendor they would share; or they heard the words of a starry-eyed rabble rouser who would create hopes he could never fill. His teaching revealed his understanding of his power, but it was not capable of generating that power in others. Words alone were inadequate to accomplish his purpose. His teaching ministry could not be the vehicle of his purpose.

Jesus decided, therefore, to supplement his teaching with specific acting out of the life-giving power of love. This is what lies behind all of the healing miracle stories of the gospel. If love can call life to fullness, it can restore that which is twisted, broken, and distorted physically and mentally. So Jesus acted. He calmed troubled minds (Mark 5:2ff), healed split personalities (Luke 8:34ff), restored sight to blind eyes (Mark 10:46), hearing to deaf ears (Mark 7:34), wholeness to broken humanity (Mark 5:25), life to dead bodies (Luke 8:41ff). But people did not see in these mighty acts the meaning of love and the Christpower was not born in them. At best they saw a wonder-worker who could give them status, so they attempted to make him king. At worst they saw a man who was demon-possessed. "By the power of Beelzebub he casts out demons" (Luke 11:15), they charged. His healing acts failed as the means of achieving his purpose, just as his teaching had failed.

Undaunted, I think, Jesus looked for still another way. He withdrew from the crowds and spent his time in intimate association with his disciples. Perhaps what they could not hear in his words or see in his deeds they could experience in a deep and open sharing of his life. So he concentrated on his disciples. This is what lies behind the farewell discourses of John (John 13–17) and the journey section of Luke (Luke 9:51–19:27). The Transfiguration was an initial dawning of understanding, at least for the inner three, Peter, James, and John; but, it was not complete. The healing of the blind man from Bethsaida (Mark 8:22ff) may well have been a parable on the response of the disciples, for sight was not given instantaneously. First there was the hazy vision that seemed like trees walking. Much more had to occur before the vision was whole.

Jesus could not overcome the disciples' insecurity even by sharing his deepest being. They used him as an ego-crutch to feed their own need for importance. They argued among themselves as to who would be the greatest (Mark 9:34). They schemed to get the upper hand, as when James and John came secretly to inquire whether they might be "secretary of state" and "secretary of defense," one to sit on his right and one on his left in his kingdom (Mark 10:35ff). Finally, when the moment of decision came the disciples proved they had not "heard" his being at all. Of the chosen twelve, one betrayed him, one denied him, and the other ten forsook him and fled. Jesus looked for a response, for a hint of recognition, for the birth of his power of love in them, but it was not forthcoming. Slowly there came upon him the realization that the response he sought would not be forthcoming, that the concentration on the disciples, the intimate attempt to share his power with them, would also fail to achieve his purpose just as did his teaching and his acts of healing.

Jesus had one other alternative. It had been his option since the moment of baptism. He had lived out his life so as never to preclude this possibility, but he had also hoped until the very end that it would not be necessary. I refer to the ancient Hebrew image of the Servant figure of Second Isaiah, a figure who willingly walked the lonely path of suffering and shame in order to bring peace, healing, and liberty to life. Jesus was true to that role and yet always held open the possibility that before the final showdown and the inevitable death of the Servant, someone would see, respond, and experience his power, thus making the final chapter unnecessary.

The door on that possibility was all but shut by the time of the Last Supper; but still he reached out to these disciples, searching for response, for understanding (Luke 22:14ff). They spent their time protesting their loyalty and their bravery. John's Gospel says Jesus assumed the literal servant's role of washing their feet (John 13:1–11), but still they could not and did not understand. Ears can be deafened to reality by ego needs. His last effort came in the Garden of Gethsemane (Mark 14:32ff). He took with him his three closest followers, Peter, James, and John. He reached out to share with them the intense agony of that hour. It was the final moment, when every other possibility faded and only the Servant's path through death to vindication remained. Those to whom he looked for response went to sleep. There was great pathos in the words "Could ye not watch with me one brief hour?" (Mark 14:37).

But there was also resolute determination when he said, "Enough! The hour has come. Up, let us go forward" (Mark 14:41–42). The path of the Servant it would be. Jesus would go through death to glory. He would lead the new exodus, from bondage into life. He would act out love in his own being in the face of every human distortion of love. The Servant role now was inescapable. It involved a final showdown with the forces of evil in Jerusalem.

In retrospect no other possibility was ever real. Jesus had prepared for this moment from the very beginning, but he had hoped it would not be necessary. The echoes of this inner debate are clearly evident in the gospel account, leading many a reader to a state of confusion.

To keep this option open he had "set his face" toward Jerusalem (Luke 9:51). He had organized the Palm Sunday procession (Luke 19:28ff). He had ridden into Jerusalem like a king, deliberately acting out a popular messianic expectation (Luke 19:35ff; Zech. 9:9–12). He had struck the ecclesiastical power structure in the heart of its vested interest, the financial rewards of the Temple trade (Luke 19:45ff). He had claimed the Temple for God, quoting, as we noted earlier, the words of Second Isaiah. He had deliberately retreated from Jerusalem to a sanctuary in Bethany on Sunday night, Monday night, Tuesday night, and Wednesday night (Mark 11:11; Mark 14:1–3). He had deliberately refused to retreat on Thursday night (Mark 14:12ff). He shared the Last Supper with his disciples (Mark 14:17ff). He set in motion at that final meal the Judas act of betrayal, the Peter act of denial, the disciples' act of fleeing (Luke 22:14–35). He went to the garden where arrest was a certainty. It was the Servant's path he walked. His decision was to give himself in the ultimate act of love. He would live love out in the face of every human distortion of love. Perhaps then people would see.

When he was betrayed, he responded by loving the betrayer, Judas. When he was denied, he responded by loving the denier, Peter. When he was forsaken, he responded by reaching out in love to the forsaking disciples. He poured out his love on the soldiers who tortured him and on the mob who screamed for his blood. He showed the freedom that love brings, even as his life was being taken away. There was no scream of the self-centered life grasping at its own being. His concern was for others. To the soldiers who drove the nails, he spoke the word of forgiveness (Luke 23:34). To the fearful penitent thief, he spoke the word of hope and assurance (Luke 23:43). To his distraught mother, he spoke the word of caring and concern (John 19:26–28). This was the free life, the whole life, the affirmed life. This was the power of love dramatically and totally acted out. What he could not accomplish through words, deeds, or in the intimate community of the disciple band he now lived out hoping that his disciples would look at his true being, see who he was, experience the power of his love, and thus find "the glorious liberty of the children of God" (Rom. 8:21).

The perfectly loved life alone can give perfect love. The totally fulfilled life alone can pour out total other-directed caring. The whole person alone can bring complete life and love and being to the world. That life alone speaks to the deepest need within us all, the need to know that we are loved just as we are; the need to be assured that there is nothing we can be and nothing we can do that finally places us outside love. If the disciples did not see this in the cross, then—like his words, his deeds, and his association with the disciples—the cross also would have failed to accomplish his purpose. The path of the Servant would have produced only the mocking silence of defeat. Jesus would not have accomplished the Messianic role. The freeing, life-giving power of love that gave him his being would not have gone beyond him. He would have lived and died in vain. In taking the Servant's path, Jesus placed the fate of his life into the hands of the disciples. They and they alone could render his life meaningless. God would not violate their consciousness and force a new conclusion. This was the realization that came to Jesus as he called to mind on the cross the twenty-second psalm and uttered those poignant words, "My God, my God, why hast thou forsaken me?" (Mark 15:34). Yet the Servant figure in Second Isaiah died in the confidence of an ultimate vindication. Jesus seemed to have the same confidence in his final utterance before death: "It is finished" (John 19:30). "Father, into thy hands I commend my spirit, my being, my purpose, my life" (Luke 23:46).

Easter is many things to me, but at the very least[7] it is the moment when it finally dawned upon the disciples who Jesus was and what the secret of his power was and is; and when they saw, they experienced the transforming birth of that life-giving power in themselves. They were grasped by love, set free by love, fulfilled by love. They were made whole. The quality of the life of Jesus became the quality of their lives. Their need to search for ego-fulfillment disappeared. Peter no longer needed to brag or impress (John 15:5ff). The disciples did not need to use people in their quest for gratification. Their fear for their own security vanished. They abandoned their upper room of hiding and became agents of life and love in the world (Acts 2). Their sense of racial or religious exclu-

clusiveness evaporated (Acts 11:5ff). They discovered that
the language of life-giving love was universal and understood by all people (Acts 2:5–13). They knew with existential certainty that life was stronger than death, and
that love was stronger than hatred. They experienced
Christpower freeing them to be, and they came alive to
their own deepest reality. They knew the meaning of Jesus' resurrection, for when they knew the affirmation that
was in him, they themselves were resurrected, transformed, converted. True to their Lord, they did not become religious; they, rather, became free to be and free
to love, free to give and free to care. The power present
in Jesus of Nazareth was now present in them. They had
life, and this life and love they were determined to share.
In this determination the mission of the Christian Church
was born. To the universal human need for love came the
universal gift of love from the Source of love seen in a
concrete, historic life.

The Christian community of the first century had no
other words or concepts in which to describe this unearthly power except the unearthly vocabulary of the first
century. So they wrote that in Jesus, God had come down
to reconcile (II Cor. 5:19). Human life alone could not
produce Jesus' power, so they asserted that his origin was
from beyond this world (John 1). They told of his birth
to a virgin mother. This was their way of explaining why
human categories could not contain him (Luke 1, 2; Matt.
1, 2). They told of his living, his dying, his descending,
his resurrecting, and his ascending. These were the words
dictated by the mind-set of the century in which this experience of love became a reality in human history.

The explanatory packaging is not relevant to our day,
but the experience of brokenness and our need for love is
still the universal human condition. The power seen in Jesus is still our deepest yearning, our eternal hope. The

experience of being healed, made whole, is still the meaning of conversion. To bring perfect affirming love is still to save.

For our day, perhaps, it would be sufficient to say that in Jesus of Nazareth we see in a human life the secret of the universe, the life-giving power of perfect love. To know this love is to know the deepest ground of being. It is to know God. It is to be at one with life's ultimate source, where freedom, rest, peace, and joy are the inevitable by-products.

The mark of the Christian is not piety but love; not religious zeal but outgoing sensitivity. It is having the power to know and accept the selves we are and the courage to be the selves we are. Dietrich Bonhoeffer, aware of this meaning, could write in his prison letters that to be a Christian is not to be "a religious person," it is simply to be a person. The full person—open, free, whole, outgoing, caring—is what it means to be Christian.

I see this Christian meaning in the comic-strip character Popeye, who gulps his spinach, flexes his muscles, and announces "I yam who I yam." He is not bragging or apologizing; he is, with rare self-acceptance, rejoicing in his being. Paul said it more gracefully, but no more profoundly: "By the grace of God I am who I am" (I Cor. 15:10).

Christians are the ones who can escape the bondage of sin and share life and love. They are the ones who have been set free by love. They see this love in the historic life of Jesus of Nazareth and so they call this life "Lord." They understand what this life meant when he said "I have come that you might have life and that you might have it abundantly." (John 10:10)

When I look at this Jesus through these Hebrew eyes, there is no ecstatic word that I cannot utter in reference to this life. In him I see Christ, Saviour, Son of the Living God; and I worship him by living, loving, and being.

16

❖

My Christ—
A Concluding Word

NEARLY two thousand years ago a man was born in an obscure village in a conquered, downtrodden country of the Roman Empire. He grew to maturity without ever leaving the land of his birth, a nation about the size of Massachusetts. He was not learned by our standards; he spoke none of the great languages of the day, only Aramaic. He earned his living as a carpenter. His close associates were social outcasts, prostitutes, tax collectors, fishermen. He established a reputation as a teacher. Stories of strange power grew up around him. Finally, he involved himself in tense conflict with the religious hierarchy. They had him arrested, tried, sentenced, tortured, and executed. They thought they had finished with him.

But from that life there emanated power, love, and life such as the world has never known. In this life many people found community, hope, the overwhelming need to give and to share, the freedom and the courage to be. The influence stemming from this life has repeatedly leaped out of the formal tradition to fuel reform movements to which the institutional church was insensitive.

His presence can be found in the fight to end slavery, the march for civil rights, and the quest for peace. Whenever the world begins to think his power is disappearing, his influence breaks forth again in strange new forms.

Around this life legends grew, superstition accrued. Men and women, groping for the power to express what they found in him, discovered the inadequacy of language, and so they lapsed into myth and poetry. All of these things together produced the Christian story that this volume has investigated.

There is nothing sacred about the words I have used. My concepts are no more eternal than were those of anyone in a previous generation. The next generation will have to repeat the process for its own time.

It has been my purpose to lay before you, my reader, a Christ, Jesus of Nazareth, and let you feel his power, gaze at his being, hear his words, and experience his gift of life. In this process it has been my hope that you might first see yourself as you are and then see yourself as you are in him, thus forcing your decision as to who it is you really want to be. I hope that you have been compelled to a serious decision—to respond to a real Christ or to give up the stereotyped religious facade. To respond to this Christ is costly, for it means being open to the new person you are in him. For, to me, Christ and life are inseparable categories and together they make worship an inescapable, glorious pleasure.

The worship of this Christ does not turn me into a pious or religious person, and I trust it will not so turn you. I cannot worship the Christ who fulfilled every human aspiration without also embracing the world gladly, as he did; or without walking into the future beyond every conventional frontier, as he walked. I cannot stand in awe of the freedom and wholeness in this Christ and not seek to break every tie that binds me or any other human being into anything less than full humanity. My worship demands that I be willing to contend against prejudice, bigotry, fear, or whatever else warps and denies another's personhood. Worship of this Christ is thus for me a call to life, to love, to compassion, to sensitivity, and to the quest for justice. It is a call to the risks of involvement and confrontation with every human being. To worship this Christ is to celebrate the present life and to hope for fulfillment that must lie beyond this life.

Here I stand. This is what Christ means to me. This Christ I discover in Jesus of Nazareth. Here I find my vocation, my life-style, my passions, and even my priesthood—a priesthood in which I am convinced every Christian must share, for it is the privilege and duty of all believers.

There will be those who will find this description of Jesus the Christ ever so inadequate; some may even call it heresy. That does not disturb me, for this enables me to live and to love, to worship and to pray as an honest man in the twentieth century. What I affirm about life I know because I have dared to trust this Christ enough to run the risk of living and loving, of being open and honest. The power that frees me to be is the power that I see in Jesus, so he is for me Lord, Saviour, Christ—a Christ who said to his disciples: "I have come that you might have life and have it abundantly"; a Christ who said: "By this shall people know that you are my disciples; not that you pass the test of traditional orthodoxy, but that you love; and in loving bear witness that you can give of the life that you have received."

I share this Christ with you in the hope that Christ might draw you into worship and into life as he has drawn me.

I close by wishing my readers "Shalom." This is about the only Hebrew word still used in our language. It is a profound word that we have debased by equating it simplistically with the Latin phrase *pax vobiscum*, "Peace go with you." It does mean peace, but in a very deep sense. Literally it should be translated "may you be whole," that is, "may you be one with yourself, with your neighbor, and with your God," for this is the essence of peace to the Hebrews.

Shalom to you through the one I call the Christ.

Notes

CHAPTER 1

1. The resolution of this area of my life is now published under the title *Honest Prayer* (Seabury, 1973).

2. I chose Luke because this gospel brings together three primary sources representing the gathered tradition of three early centers of Christianity. Biblical scholars identify Mark with Rome, Quelle with Ephesus, and "L" with Caesarea. Those who accept the proto-Luke theory as I do would maintain that Luke combined "Q" and "L" into a gospel narrative that antedates Mark. This narrative they would contend was expanded and enriched by the addition of Markan material somewhere in the decade between 80 and 90 C.E.

CHAPTER 2

1. John Taylor, in his book *The Go-Between God,* makes this point in relation to the Holy Spirit: "It is vital for our understanding of the Holy Spirit to recognize that the spirit in a man is not the most rarefied element, lying beyond 'mind' in the spectrum of his being. It is the power of his personhood which holds body and mind in unity. We, who suffer from the long unnatural divorce we have imposed upon the two, need desperately to learn that the Holy Spirit is just as likely to speak through our bodies as through our minds." *The Go-Between God,* John V. Taylor, Fortress Press, Philadelphia, 1973, p. 50.

2. This writer of a major strand of the Hebrew scriptures is so called because his name for God is *Yahweh*.

3. The priestly writer was the author of another strand of material in the Hebrew scriptures. The "priestly writer" probably meant a group rather than a person, and the work was completed after the exile. It is marked with a very ritualistic, ecclesiastical flavor. Most of the minutiae of our Jewish law came from this source.

4. For a fuller explanation of what lies behind Adam's naming of the animals, see *Honest Prayer,* John S. Spong, Seabury Press, New York, 1973, p. 48.

5. I am aware of the debate in biblical circles as to whether the children of Israel went through the Red Sea or the Sea of Reeds. Though I side with the advocates of the Sea of Reeds, the point is not germane to this volume.

CHAPTER 3

1. Scholars debate whether or not *creatio ex nihilo* is in fact a proper reading of the Hebrew text. They suggest that it is highly unlikely that the ancient Hebrews could have had so philosophical a base. This particular account in Genesis is from the hand of the priestly writer and the issue can be argued. However, the affirmation of the priestly writer is finally to the goodness of life, including physical material reality. God saw "all that he made, and behold, it was good."

2. In 597 B.C.E. the Hebrew nation of Judah was overrun and conquered by the Babylonians. In accordance with Babylonian policy a massive shifting of population took place. The Jews were taken to Babylon and resettled there. This became known as the exile. A key figure in the exile was Ezekiel, who shaped the thought patterns of the Hebrew people and turned them toward external piety. From the time of the exile the "good" person did come to be identified with the externally "religious" person. Fed by Ezra and Nehemiah, the exact keeping of the law in minute detail became synonymous with goodness. This attitude finally produced the Pharisees of Jesus' day. Jesus, in the true tradition of the Hebrew prophets, attacked this with a fervor that had been unknown in Israel for centuries. In the true Hebrew tradition worship and life could never be divided.

3. The exact date is, of course, speculative. But most estimates are no earlier than 8 B.C.E. and no later than 4 B.C.E. The Bethlehem tradition is also under serious question.

4. One of the major earlier antecedents was the religion of Persia called Zoroastrianism. The Hebrews encountered dualism while in exile, and they began to reflect the dualistic influence from that day on so that the categories do, in fact, begin to blur. For further references I would suggest Rudolf Bultmann's book *Primitive Christianity in Its Contemporary Setting,* translated by R. H. Fuller (New York, The World Publishing Co., 1956); also Martin Buber's *Two Types of Faith,* translated by N. P. Goldhawk (New York, Harper & Row, 1961).

5. This subject was treated in detail in my book entitled *Beyond Moralism,* coauthored with Denise G. Haines published in 1986 by Harper & Row.

CHAPTER 5

1. My authority for this statement is J. Jeremias's *The Lord's Prayer,* Biblical Series, Philadelphia, Fortress Press, 1964. I developed his point of view in Chapter II of *Honest Prayer,* Seabury Press, 1973.

2. Sigmund Freud in his book *Moses and Monotheism* suggested that Moses was, in fact, the illegitimate son of Pharaoh's daughter by a Hebrew servant, and that his choosing to make his identification with the Hebrew slave people, when he could have chosen the regal life of the royal court, was the human experience which the Hebrews used to understand and articulate their sense of being God's chosen people.

CHAPTER 6

1. I am aware that the primary purpose of this biblical episode was to determine which deity could produce rain and thus be the source of fertility. However, the fire detail is the focus for our purposes.

CHAPTER 7

1. Scholars differ as to just how much of chapters 40 to 66 of our Book of Isaiah is the work of Second Isaiah, and whether or

not there was a Third Isaiah, but that debate is not germane to this book, for Jesus related to it as one cohesive source.

2. Dr. Fleming James.

CHAPTER 8

1. Though many scholars disagree that Isaiah 56–66 is a part of Second Isaiah, Jesus made no such distinction, so it was influenced by the entirety of the volume.

CHAPTER 15

1. Nestorius (c. 450) taught that there were two separate persons in Jesus, one divine, the other human. They were joined, but not into a single union.

2. Apollinarius (c. 350) taught that in humanity there coexists body, mind, and spirit. In Christ, however, spirit was not human but taken over by the divine logos, and Christ was therefore not completely human.

3. Arius (c. 300) taught that the Son was created by the Father and was therefore not God by nature.

4. Either the Apostles' Creed or the Nicene Creed.

5. I know of no biblical scholar who treats the birth narratives as history.

6. When this book was originally conceived, I had planned to devote one unit to the interpretive envelope in which the gospel story was carried: the birth narrative on the one side and the resurrection on the other. But so massive was the material I gathered that I decided to save it for a future publication. Suffice it to say here that I believe the story of the virgin birth was a theological interpretation required by the historic fact of the resurrection. A fuller exposition of this statement must await the future work.

7. I hope my readers note the words "very least," for there is a great deal more that I believe Easter is. I have explored this in detail in my book *The Easter Moment,* Harper & Row, 1980, 1987.

Bibliography

Brown, Raymond F.: *The Birth of the Messiah,* Doubleday, New York, 1977.

Buber, Martin: *Two Types of Faith,* Harper & Row, New York, 1961. Tr. by N. P. Goldhawk.

Bultmann, Rudolf. *Primitive Christianity in its Contemporary Setting,* World Publishing Co., New York, 1956. Tr. R. H. Fuller.

Caird, G. B.: *St. Luke,* Pelican Series, Penguin Books, Philadelphia, 1963.

Campbell, Joseph: *The Hero with a Thousand Faces,* Bollingen Series, Princeton University Press, Princeton, 1949.

Conzelmann, Hans: *The Theology of St. Luke,* Harper & Row, New York, 1960.

Cox, Harvey: *The Secular City,* Macmillan, New York, 1966.

Ellis, E. Earle: *The Gospel of Luke,* New Century Bible, Thos. Nelson & Son, Camden, 1966.

Freud, Sigmund, ed. Katherine Jones: *Moses and Monotheism,* Random House, New York, 1955.

Harris, Thomas: *I'm OK, You're OK,* Harper & Row, New York, 1967.

Hoskyns, Edwin C.: *The Fourth Gospel,* Faber & Faber, London, 1940.

James, Fleming: *Personalities of the Old Testament*, Charles Scribner's Sons, New York, 1951.

Joachim, Jeremias: *The Lord's Prayer*, Fortress Press, Philadelphia, 1964.

May, Rollo: *Love and Will*, W. W. Norton & Company, New York, 1969.

May, Rollo: *Power and Innocence*, W. W. Norton & Company, New York, 1972.

Nineham, D. E.: *St. Mark*, Pelican Series, Penguin Books, Baltimore, 1963.

Robinson, John A. T.: *Honest to God*, Westminster Press, Philadelphia, 1963.

Robinson, John A. T.: *The Human Face of God*, Westminster Press, Philadelphia, 1973.

Spong, John S.: *The Easter Moment*, Harper & Row, San Francisco and New York, 1980 and 1987.

Spong, John S.: *Honest Prayer*, Seabury Press, New York, 1973.

Spong, John S.: *Into the Whirlwind*, Harper & Row, San Francisco and New York, 1983.

Spong, John S., and Haines, Denise G.: *Beyond Moralism*, Harper & Row, San Francisco and New York, 1986.

Tate, L. Gordon: *The Promise of Tillich*, J. B. Lippincott Co., New York, 1971.

Taylor, John V.: *The Go-Between God*, Fortress Press, Philadelphia, 1973.

Temple, William: *Readings in St. John*, Macmillan, New York, 1945.

Von Rad, Gerhard: *Genesis—A Commentary*, Westminster Press, Philadelphia, 1961.